I0040098

THE FUNDAMENTALS OF
BUYING AND SELLING COMPANIES

Published in 2008 by
Corporate Turnaround Centre Pte Ltd.

Printed in Singapore
by Markono Print Media Pte Ltd.

9 8 7 6 5 4 3 2 1
09   08

Copyright ⓐ 2008 by Corporate Turnaround Centre Pte Ltd. All
rights reserved. This publication is protected by Copyright and
permission should be obtained from the publisher prior to any
prohibited reproduction, storage in a retrieval system, or transmission in
any form or by any means, electronic, mechanical, photocopying,
recording, or likewise. For information regarding permission(s), write
to: miketeng@pacific.net.sg.

Table of Contents

Background of the trainer

Dr Michael Teng is the author of the book *"Corporate Turnaround: Nursing a sick company back to health",* in 2002 which is also translated into the Bahasa Indonesia. It was one of the top selling management books then. In 2006, he authored another book entitled, *"Corporate Wellness: 101 Principles in Turnaround and Transformation."* He also published in 2007/2008 four books, namely entitled: *Internet Turnaround: The Use of Internet Marketing to Turnaround Companies ; Training Manual: Corporate Turnaround and Transformation Methodology*; *Link Baiting to Improve Your Page Ranking on Search Engines and Corpoate Turnaround: Global Perspective.*

He is the first Asian speaker to be featured on SuccessUniversity.com, which is the world's most visited website on personal development. Dr Teng is also the top five author of BuildYourOwnBusiness.com in 2006.

He has been interviewed on the national media on many occasions on the subject of corporate turnaround and transformation. Dr Teng is widely recognized as an expert on corporate turnaround in Asia by the news media such as the Channel NewsAsia, News Radio FM 93.8, the Boss Magazine, Economic Bulletin, the Today, World Executive Digest, Lianhe ZaoPao, StarBiz and the Straits Times.

He has 28 years of experience in corporate turnaround, strategic planning and operational management responsibilities in the Asia Pacific region. Of these, he held Chief Executive Officer's positions for 18 years in multi-national, local and publicly listed companies. He led in the successful turnaround of several troubled companies. He is currently the Managing Director of Corporate Turnaround Centre Pte Ltd.

Dr Teng served as the Executive Council member for fourteen years and the last four years as the President of the Marketing Institute of Singapore (2000 - 2004), the national body representing individual and corporate members in Singapore. Dr Teng holds a Doctor in Business Administration (DBA) from the University of South Australia, Master in Business Administration (MBA) and Bachelor in Mechanical Engineering (BEng) from the National University of Singapore. He is also a Professional Engineer (P Eng, Singapore), Chartered Engineer (C Eng, UK) and Fellow Member of Chartered Institute of Marketing (FCIM), Chartered Management Institute (FCMI), Institute of Mechanical Engineers (FIMechE), Institute of Electrical Engineers (FIEE), Marketing Institute of Singapore (FMIS) and Senior Member of Singapore Computer Society (SMSCS).

Introduction

Everyone wants to be their own boss. The easiest way to do this is to have your own business. You can own a business and be your own boss. But to own a business, you either need to start your own business or buy an existing business. Starting a business is not for everyone but yes just about anyone and everyone can buy an existing business.

This book will guide you on how to buy an existing business for the right prices, turn around the business if the business you purchased is a sick business and how to grow your business through mergers and acquisitions. All business if managed properly will grow. However they will not grow rapidly as you may want it to. Through mergers and acquisitions, you can grow your business many folds. Once your business has grown, you may want to sell it and get back your investment and a profit. This book will also guide you on how to sell your business for the best price.

Why Buy

So why would you want to own a business? Owning your own business will let you be your own boss. It will enable you to control your financial and professional destiny. You get tremendous satisfaction. You are not longer working under a work culture. You can establish the work culture. It offers you flexibility in your working hours. You are the boss and you can tailor your work schedule to meet your personal needs. There are also some tax benefits which you can derive by owning a business.

But be warned that having your own business does not and cannot be a guarantee of your financial success. Owning a business also brings with it many responsibilities. You have to handle the pressures of the business. It may not be as easy as you may have thought it to be. There is a lot of red tape and bureaucratic hassles in owning and running a business. Add to that the taxes and employee benefits, not to mention the employee unions. Like in any business, the business that you buy will also have its competitors whose main aim will be to drive you out of business. The market for any product is ever changing. If you cannot read the pulse of the market and change or modify your product, your business may be doomed.

You have thought over it for a long time and finally decided that you want to own a business. That is the first decision you take towards buying your own business and probably the easiest decision in the entire process.

Existing Business Vs New Business

You are then faced with the option of either starting a new business or buying an existing one.

There are a number of issues you need to consider before you take your decision. Starting a new business is certainly not an easy task. It is an anguishing and painful task. To begin with, it is very difficulty to get financing for a new business, especially if it is your first business. Even if you do manage to get the necessary finance, you have a lot to do before the business becomes successful. You will need to build the business, get the customers, generate revenue and create a profit. You will also need to hire employees and managers. You will need to spend considerable time, money and effort building the business.

There are many advantages of buying an existing business over starting a new business. The most important one is that the business is already up and running. You can avoid all the pitfalls of starting a new business. It is not easy to make immediate profit from a newly started business. To make a new business successful, you will have to spend considerable time, money and efforts where in an existing business, the owner would have done all this. You will only need to make small changes in the business.

If you start a new business, there is no guarantee that you will make a profit whereas an existing business would have already proven its track record. The fact that it is an existing business adds to the value. The business is functioning and is likely to have customers. It takes a substantial amount of time and effort to build and maintain a good customer base. An existing business will have its infrastructure including customers, suppliers, employees, equipment and systems in place. All required licenses and permits for the business would have already been acquired. This will allow you to focus on building the business as opposed to a start up. An existing business will also have its own marketing and distribution set up. A well-trained sales force combined with an effective distribution system is valuable asset. The previous owner will in all likelihood lend support and goodwill to the existing business.

A newly established business will find it difficult to raise finances whereas on the other hand banks and financial institutions are more liberal when releasing funds to an existing business. The reason is that it is easier to assess the risks involved in an existing business than those in a new business. An existing business is a known quantity with an existing location, current customers, staff, suppliers and reputation. Sometimes, the seller of an existing business will finance the entire transaction if he or she has faith in you, the buyer.

Buying a business is at times less expensive that starting a new one. You can almost certainly negotiate the purchase price. You can easily investigate the past activities, operations, current status, competition, industry and future potential of an existing business as compared to setting up a new business. You can easily decide what has to be done to successfully run the business. You just need to take it further from where it is.

There is however certain downsides which you must be aware of before you buy an existing business. The major bottleneck is the cost of purchasing a new business. Sometime the purchase price could be beyond the funds you have earmarked for the purchase. At times, the cost could be greater than starting a new business. The main reasons for the high costs is that the business will have all its infrastructure in place and you will have to bear the cost of conducting a due diligence before the purchase which will involve the services of professionals such as lawyers and accountants.

When you purchase an existing business, you will be purchasing with all its assets as well as liabilities and outstanding contracts which might not be favorable to you at times. There could be inherent problems in the business and you could end up investing much more than the purchase price. Another thing you need to know is that the existing employees might not be favorable to a change in ownership. Also existing customers may shift their loyalty with a change in the ownership.

If by any chance, the existing business does not enjoy a nice image, you might find it difficult to change that. Also some of the physical assets of the company such as machinery and office equipments may be old and might need replacements.

On the whole, buying an existing business is a better deal for you especially if this is your first business. You can certainly eliminate the difficulties associated with starting a new business by buying an existing business.

Once you have decided on buying an existing business, you are then faced with the question of which is the right business for you. For you to be successful in your endeavor, it is important that you buy the business that is right for you.

The right business

When you are buying a business, it is most important that you buy the right one. It is the number one concern amongst business buyers. The simplest and the quickest way to find your own business is to buy one that you already know well. But with so many businesses around for sale, this doesn't necessarily mean that it is the "right" business for you to buy.

Your work experience, knowledge, qualifications, skills, talent and personality all play an important role in deciding the right business for you. The business should let you utilize your strong qualities to further the business. Select a business that matches your work experience, knowledge, qualifications, skills, talent and personality.

Narrowing down the choice

The key is to focus on a business that incorporates and leverages your area of expertise. You must be able to utilize your strongest talent to drive the business. There is nothing like the RIGHT business for you. It is what you make it to be after you buy it. Narrow down the list of businesses by matching them with your interests, talent, skills and personality. Ask yourself if you will be comfortable dealing with a wide range of personalities and the needs of numerous customers, or are you more comfortable interacting with a small number of clients? Can you delegate well and handle the needs and schedules of various employees, or should look for a one or two person operation? Can you handle the challenges of the around-the-clock environment, or do you prefer a business that works Monday-through-Friday? Are you comfortable maintaining an inventory, or do you prefer a service-oriented business?

Select a business that matches your interests, talent, skill and personality. You must consider your temperament, attention to detail, people skills, ability to multi-task, ability to delegate, and other personal characteristics.

Industry

Never get into a business which you know nothing about. It has all the recipes for a disaster. Owning a business in a familiar industry is tough enough. If you buy a business which you know nothing about, you will get into a situation where you have to learn how to run the business and then add in the difficulty of learning about a whole new industry. You must know beforehand the industry to which your experience and skills are best suited.

Expectations

Never have any unrealistic expectations from a business. Be realistic. You must consider what you want from the business. Always consider if the business will give you a chance to improve your life and build something big and how it will impact the lives of others, especially the near and dear ones. Don't ever try to run a business into a hobby. It's bound to fail.

Sacrifices

Remember behind every successful business is a lot of sacrifices. If you want your business to succeed, be prepared for sacrifices. Nothing comes without a price. The reward is proportional to the sacrifice. You have to make sacrifices in order to buy and build a business

You are buying a business because you have certain expectations from it. To make the business meet those expectations, you must be ready for sacrifices. Don't confuse sacrifices with restrictions. Sacrifices need to be made, but only because of the rewards.

Experience

Your experience, skills, talent and personality are all very important factors in deciding the right business. Choose the business that suits your experience, skills, talent and personality. Do not try to change your experience, skills, talent and personality to suit the business after you buy it. Make sure that you buy a business that you enjoy doing. It is fundamental and important to the success of the business. Of equal importance is to note what you do not enjoy. Some businesses may require that you do it yourself. Make sure this isn't what drives the business and be certain that you can hire or outsource for this function. Target businesses where you have experience in the driving force of the business and not just an interest.

Strength

Match your strengths to the requirements of the business. Choose an existing business type that fits the strengths that you have and won't suffer too badly from your weaknesses.

Restrictions and Weakness

Consider certain restrictions that you may have on yourself which could hinder the successful operation of the business. Never get into a situation where a particular business may cause irreparable harm to something that is infinitely more important than a business. You must know your weaknesses. Consider them in relation to the business. Your weaknesses may do yourself terrible harm when choosing a business. Be clear and be critical. Do not buy a business if your weaknesses are where the business needs strengths.

Market position

Does the business have an existing market? If no, then would you be able to create a market? Does the business enjoy exclusivity? Do the finished products have a demand in the market? These are important factors to be considered. You do not want to buy a business whose products do not have a market. If there is no market, the business will be a failure. Consider the existing and likely competitors for the business. If there is cut throat competition, stay away from that business.

Product

In business, nothing happens unless someone sells something. Once you own a business, you will have to sell its product if the business is to be successful. There is no substitution for great product. You must know the product flawlessly and sell the benefits it delivers. Deal honestly with the customers. This is very important for the success of the business.

Finance

The finance and other resources available with you is a very important factor in deciding the right business to buy. You need not have the entire money at your disposal. Banks and financial institutions will gladly help you and finance the purchase. However the business has to be attractive enough for the banks and financial institutions to finance the deal. Also sometimes, the seller will be willing to finance the sale.

You may have decided which is the right business for you. But then you have to locate the right business. It just doesn't come to you. You need to find it.

Resources for locating the right business

Once you decide on the right business for yourself, the question arises - How do you find this business? Just as you wouldn't buy a house after looking at only one, you mustn't buy a business immediately upon hearing about one available business. There are many resources available but you should not restrict yourself to one source.

Classifieds

Scrutinize the classifieds section of your newspaper. You'll find listings for a number of businesses being offered for sale. Check out all those that you find interesting. The listings will include listings by owners and by business brokers. Be careful with the listings. Some of them will be inserted only to cheat unsuspecting victims. Without verifying the authenticity of the listing and the party behind the listing, do not make any payments.

Publications

There is an incredible number of publications available which list businesses for sale. Get a local publication as it is more likely to have listings in your area. Review the listings. You will ultimately find a business that is of interest to you. You can then contact the seller or the broker who has inserted the listing.

Internet

This is an area which has a lot to offer. There are numerous sites which provide listings of businesses for sale. Some of the major sites include:
http://www. bizbuysell.com
http://www.bizquest.com
http://www.businessesforsale.com
http://www.businessbroker.net
http://www.mergerplace.com
http://www.bizsale.com

http://www.ibizseller.com
http://www.globalbx.com

The same business is sometimes listed on several sites. Most of these sites are dominated by business brokers and they place the ads everywhere. However, it's well worth to search all sites frequently.

Some of these sites may have an email alert program. Sign up for such programs. You can enter specific criteria such as type of business, location, budget, etc and whenever there is a new listing matching your criteria, you will receive an email.

Lawyers and Accountants

Lawyers and Accountants are a good source of information. Many of their clients might be interested in selling a business. Make it known to them that you are on the look out for a business to buy. Ask them if they have any clients whose business may be up for sale. Provide them with all relevant information about yourself.

Bank and Financial Institutions

Banks and Financial Institutions can be a good source for locating business that may be up for sale. The manager of a bank is the right person to contact. Let him know that you are on the look out for a business to buy and enquire if any of their customers have a business for sale. Provide all relevant information about yourself.

Chamber of Commerce

Try and become a member of a Chamber of Commerce and attend their meetings. You will get to meet business owners at such meetings and develop your contacts which can ultimately help you locate a business for sale.

Business Contacts

Your business contacts are another source for locating businesses for sale. Let them know that you are in the market. The word will spread and you might just get lucky.

Family and Friends

Let everyone and anyone who you feel has some business contact or the other know that you are looking to buy a business. You may never know. Someone within the circle might be planning to sell a business or might know someone who wants to.

Business broker

This is probably the best way to buy a business. There are many qualified business brokers out there whose main job is to act as a meeting point for buyers and sellers. It is very important that the broker is a qualified one. Most jurisdictions do not have any licensing requirements for business brokers. Look for brokers who deal exclusively in business brokerage.

Business brokers usually operate just like real estate brokers. The broker will have a series of listings gathered from numerous sellers, and it's the seller who pays the broker's commission. If you're interested in buying a type of business your broker doesn't have a listing for, he or she may be able to find such a business from another broker, and the two of them would divide the commission.

Most brokers obtain exclusive listings from their sellers, and so no broker has a complete inventory of all the businesses available. So visit as many brokers as you can. However most good brokers will lose interest in you if they find you've been visiting the others. Good brokers will work hard for you but only if they believe you've placed your trust exclusively in them. You can also work exclusively with one really good broker who will be able to find out from the other brokers what's available.

A good broker will try to find out as much as possible about you before showing you any business. Some brokers will do a lot of the things that need to be done to close the purchase of the business while others will only bring the prospective buyer and seller together and wait for their commission.

There are many advantages for using the services of a broker. The broker can show you business which you might never have found on your own. A good broker can help you keep an open mind during your search and figure out what you don't want to do and move on from there.

When you choose a broker, check on their experience, the transactions they have been involved with, their background, references and style of functioning.

They are great source of information on current market conditions, issues related to pricing and financing, and many other facets of the business buying process.[1]

They are capable of separating the buyers from the lookers, which can save you valuable time. In most cases they will get you a better price than you could on your own.

The broker has understanding of the current market and buying process, and can assist you in the pricing. The broker will have access to recent sales histories on similar businesses which help to determine an unbiased and accurate assessment of the business you want to buy.

There will be times when you will need a buffer between you and the seller. The broker can help deliver bad news to the seller. At times, you may have to retract or modify an offer or you will need to adopt an aggressive position during the negotiation. You will need the seller's assistance even after you buy the business to run the business smoothly. It is in your interest not to aggravate them too severely. So a business broker can deliver the bad news to the seller and you can avoid getting into the seller's bad books.

A good broker will be able to help put together all the paperwork involved in the purchase of a business.

Unless you hire a broker, the broker will be representing the seller.

Only you can decide which is the right business for you. Business brokers only can assist you. It is up to you to make the final decision.

---

[1] http://www.inc.com/articles/2000/10/20486.html

Locating the business is just the beginning. There is a lot left to be done for you to own the business. The first challenge you will face is dealing with the buyer.

Dealing with the Seller

The Seller plays an important role in the entire process. The Seller will be looking for a buyer. His ideal buyer would be one, who does not compete with him n his existing business, presents him with the least hassles after the sale and offers him the best or the highest price. There are chances that you may need to work with the seller for a few days even after you purchase the business to ensure smooth transitions of ownership. Make sure that the seller is someone who gets along with you. Keep your ego out of the way. You will need information from the seller on how to improve the business. Seller hindsight will be helpful deciding the future course of the business.

Negotiations

Once you have decided on which business to buy and you have contacted the seller, you will need to begin the negotiations for the purchase. Although you may want to be polite to the seller, never take the sellers word for everything.

Negotiation involves information exchange and deliberations between the seller and you towards effecting the sale. You can seek clarifications to apprehensions about the business and the seller will justify the business.

First of all, you must find out the reason for the sale. The seller may say that he is selling because he wants to retire or move out of town but there could be other reasons. The future of the business may not be so bright as the seler is painting it to be. The business may have lost its major customer who accounts for a large portion of its revenue or a major competitor is moving to town or the products of the business could be outdated. You do not want to be stuck with such a business. Hence the reason for the sale is very important and it should be your priority to find out the reason for the sale.

It is very important that you know what is included in the sale. Does it cover all the assets? Are the assets charged to any party? What are the liabilities of the business? The last thing you want is to be straddled with someone else's liability.

Once you have decided to purchase the business, it is best that you put it down in writing by sending a letter of intent to the seller. A sample letter of intent is annexed to the book.

A letter of intent outlines the agreement between you and the seller before the purchase agreement is finalized. It is the formal method of stating that you as a prospective buyer are interested in purchasing the business. It officially declares that the two of you are negotiating the sale of the business. It will also provide certain safeguards in case the negotiations fail. However a letter of intent is not an offer and does not create any obligation on the parties.

Once you have sent the letter of intent and it has been accepted by the seller, you can officially begin what is probably the most important stage in the entire process: Due diligence.

Due Diligence

There is very little statutory protection for the purchaser of a business. Some jurisdictions do have remedies which may entitle the buyer to damages and/or sue for misrepresentation. The purpose of due diligence is to assist you as the buyer to find out everything you reasonably can including the factors critical to the success of the business including its strengths and weaknesses.

Due diligence is a term used for a number of concepts involving the performance of an investigation of a business. It commonly applies to voluntary investigations. In particular, due diligence is a process through which a potential buyer evaluates a target business for purchase.

The main purpose of due diligence is to allow you to find out everything that you need to know about the business and it will allow you to consider your options in light of the facts. If the due diligence unearths information that makes the purchase risky or undesirable and the defects cannot be adequately resolved, then you can withdraw from the negotiations. You can also negotiate the purchase price based on the findings of your due diligence. If you find any problems with the business, you can inform the seller and have them fixed.

You can purchase the business based on the representations of the seller. However in such cases, if things go wrong after the purchase, you will have to resort to litigation to get your money back. It is therefore advantageous to identify the problem before hand rather than relying on the seller's representations.

You should hire the services of lawyers and accountants to conduct the due diligence for you. Due diligence is best left to professionals as it is a very complicated task and it is probably the most important process in the purchase of an existing business. It is best to let your accountants do the financial and tax due diligence while your lawyers do the others. The final report should be a joint project with accountants and lawyers. Accountants will have the necessary knowledge of accounting and tax principles. Lawyers will be able to analyse the documents, contracts, licenses and permits of the business.

Independent Verification

While you are conducting due diligence, you must also conduct an independent verification by checking public records. Conducting a search at the Registrar of Companies will reveal all particulars about articles and memorandum of association, share capital, directors, registered office, charges over assets, etc.

Approach credit agencies to obtain information about the business' credit worthiness. A bankruptcy search must be made over each of the directors or against individual sellers to determine whether any petition in bankruptcy, receiving order or deed of arrangement has been registered.

You should also conduct litigation search to establish whether the business has any judgment or winding-up petition entered against it.

If the business claims to be a member of a trade organization or has a special accreditation, then you should check with the concerned trade organization or accreditation body. If the business professes to adhere to a code of practice, then check with the relevant body that it has done so. If the business requires special licenses, check whether the license is still in force and whether your purchase of the business will affect such license.

Conducting due diligence

You can begin the due diligence by requesting information from the seller. Sometimes the seller may require you to sign a confidentiality agreement. The sale of an on-going business is very confidential for both the seller and the prospective buyer. All inquiries are held in strict confidence. Meetings and information shared or observed are to be held in strict confidence.

The extent of information you will need will depend upon the nature of the business and the amount you want to invest. However the following information must be looked into during any due diligence:

1. Formation documents including memorandum and articles of association should be reviewed to determine the seller's power to consummate the transaction and for potential impediments including any rights of first refusal.

2. Audited accounts for the last three years and subsequent unaudited and management accounts, details of share capital

3. Minutes of director's and shareholders meetings

4. Details of licenses and permits required for the business

5. Details of all borrowings of the business including a schedule of all indebtedness of the business, instruments evidencing the indebtedness, guarantees, letter of credit, etc

6. Particulars of any pending and threatened litigation, arbitrations and government investigations.

7. Details of employees, including name, address, age, date of joining, salary, other allowances, job position, disciplinary action, if any.

8. Details of all contracts signed

9. Details of all taxes paid and payable, pending and likely tax disputes

10. Particulars of all insurance and insurance claims outstanding.

11. Title to assets

12. Details of the properties owned and leased, rent, mortgages, encumbrances on property

13. Intellectual Property rights of the business.

14. Management structure of the business

15. Description of the business, methods of operation, sales and marketing policies, major suppliers and customers, market share. n

Once you have all these information, you can begin the due diligence.

An important area of due diligence relates to employees. The employment terms of all employees must be checked carefully and in particular the service agreements of the directors and other key staff. Verify the notice period for termination of the services. As a minimum, you must ascertain the salary and other allowances of the employees, whether the business has been engaged in discriminatory practices or whether the business has provided the necessary benefits to the employees as required by law.

The property of the business is yet another important area of due diligence. In addition to verifying the document to title, you must make a physical examination of the property.

You should conduct appropriate searches at the land registry to establish whether there are any adverse encumbrances, obligations or restrictions on the property. In the case of a leasehold property, you may inherit continuing as well as future liabilities for breaches of the lease. You should therefore ensure that the landlord has not commenced any forfeiture proceedings and that there is no outstanding liability for dilapidations arising from the seller's failure to repair and that the rent has been paid up to date.

Check if the termination clause of the lease. Sometimes you may require the landlord's consent before the lease can be assigned to you.

Check the rent review clause of the lease. The profitability of the business can be radically affected by an adverse rent review.

Financial due diligence of the business is necessary for an independent assessment of the business and its financial information. Hire accountants to do this job for you. Meet with the accountants before drawing up the terms of reference in order to establish a realistic time frame and to agree the costs. You should liaise between your accountants doing the financial due diligence and your lawyers who are looking into the other aspects of due diligence. This will ensure that you do not waste time and money in duplicating the due diligence and that all areas are covered within the time frame. The main objective of the financial due diligence is to obtain specific financial, commercial, administrative information regarding the business including but not limited to the following:

1. constitution and structure of the business
2. capital structure of the business
3. shareholding pattern
4. shareholder rights
5. current position of assets and liabilities of the business
6. summary of latest net asset position
7. review of financial position including financing arrangements, working capital requirements, contingent liabilities
8. summary of the last three years profit and loss account
9. accounting policies
10. tax affairs of the business

Nowadays, environmental due diligence has become an essential component of due diligence. There are a number of reasons why environmental liabilities are relevant to your purchase:

a) The control over certain business activities which can affect the environment are increasing by the day and becoming more complex
b) Insurance against environmental liabilities is difficult to obtain.
c) Public opinion
d) Under the existing laws, liability for violation of an environmental law will fall on the original polluter who has knowingly permitted the polluting material to remain in the land. However if such persons cannot be found, the present owner or occupier may become liable to carry out remedial measures which can be very expensive and thus affect the bottom line of the business.

Environmental due diligence is necessary to determine the extent and the nature of risk involved in buying a business and becoming responsible for its liabilities. You must make sure that the business complies with all the environmental regulations and has all necessary permits and clearance from the relevant authorities for carrying on the business.

Your accountants must investigate the tax position of the business. Verifying the accuracy of the information is essential. The main purpose of a tax due diligence is to determine the existence of any potential exposure to a tax liability.

Another purpose of tax due diligence is to ensure that the valuation of the business can be properly ascertained. Tax due diligence will establish whether the business' tax affairs are currently in order and whether there could be any sudden tax liabilities which could arise in the near future.

Use the tax due diligence to identify the tax saving opportunities that you can take advantage of after you buy the business.

The extent of due diligence you conduct is based on many factors, including the size of the transaction, the likelihood of closing a transaction, tolerance for risk, time constraints, cost factors, and resource availability. It is impossible to learn everything about a business but it is important to learn enough such that you lower your risks to the acceptable levels and make good, informed business decisions.

Time allocated for due diligence can vary widely with each situation. Time schedules through the closing of a business purchase transaction are typically tight. You should ensure that adequate time is allocated to due diligence. Maintain confidentiality of all information that you have access to during due diligence.

When you are conducting due diligence, it is also necessary that you should have the most important resource necessary to own the business – finance. All your efforts of dealing with the seller and conducting the due diligence will be a waste of time and money if you haven't lined up your finances. You won't get far in your endeavour of buying and owning a business without finance.

Raising Finance

Before you embark on buying a business, you must make sure that you have the finances ready. Your personal finances are your best source for financing the deal. However if you cannot finance the entire deal from your own pocket, you need not worry. There are other avenues from where you can raise the money necessary to finance the deal.

Banks & Finance Companies

This is the most common option for raising funds. Banks and finance companies will be willing to give you loans to finance the purchase.

Loans are mainly of two types:

1. Business Loans
2. Consumer Loans

Business loans are secured with business or personal assets. Business loans have strict requirements. Banks and finance companies will usually ask for personal guarantees, as well as collateral from you. If after you buy the business, the business happens to be in tough financial times, the bank of finance company may ask you to immediately pay off the full amount of the loan.

You can finance the purchase of the business through personal or other loans based on personal assets. Consumer and personal loans are easier to obtain than business loans. Most banks and finance companies do not mind if you take a consumer loan from them and use the funds to finance your purchase. All you need is a healthy credit history. Personal and consumer loans require less paperwork.

Finance companies are willing to take more risks as compared to banks. However their costs may also be higher than banks.

Venture Capital Funds

Venture capital is a type of private equity capital typically provided by outside investors for financing of new, growing or struggling businesses. Venture capital investments generally are high risk investments but offer the potential for above average returns and/or a percentage of ownership of the business.

There are many venture capitalists who are willing to invest in various businesses. They invest and provide money in sums ranging from $250,000 to $10 million or more. Most venture capitalists have set limits, minimums, and maximums they are willing to invest, and some specialize in an industry or certain regions.

Before investing in a business, venture capitalists will look into the growth prospects of the business and the management talent. You will need to provide them with a lot of information including a business plan. There is no fixed standard. Each venture capitalist has its own set of rules. However you need to beware of frauds. Some fraudsters pose as venture capitalists and ask for some upfront payment and then disappear with your money.

Angel Investors

Angel investors are people with money and are looking for investments. They seek a better return than traditional investments. They provide sums of money in the under $200,000 range and tend to invest in their geographical regions. They pay great importance to the growth and revenue potential of the business. They usually seek an equity in return for the financing but are not interested in running the business.

Friends and Family

Although friends and family can be a source of funds to finance your purchase, they are best avoided. Use them only as the last resort. You risk your relationship with them by borrowing from them.

Seller Financing

In the United States and in some other jurisdictions, most business purchases, especially small business purchases involve seller purchase. In the event of the seller financing the purchase, you will have to sign a guarantee the repayment. However you need to pledge any personal assets as collateral.

Grants

There are many governmental and private organizations that provide grants to entrepreneurs. Certain local and state governments also provide such grants.

You may arrange the finances from which source you may find it or from which source that is ready to finance your purchase. However make sure that you will be able to repay them. If you fail to, they can come after the very business that you purchased using their money.

How much finance you will need depends on the valuation of the business. Don't rely on the seller's valuation. It will in all probability be an inflated one. Sellers just want to get the maximum out of their business. To make sure that you are protected, it is important that you carry out your own valuation to ensure that you are paying a reasonable price for the business.

Valuation

Before you make purchase the business, you need to determine the value of the business to make the best offer. The price the seller may quote will not be the right price. To determine the right price, you will need to conduct a valuation of the business.

Valuation is an important aspect in your purchase process. It should be done by a team of experts taking into consideration the objectives of your purchase. Your team of experts should compromise of accountants, financial experts and technical experts who can look into the aspects of valuation from different angles. Technical experts have their own role in the valuation process to look into the life and validity of depreciated assets and replacements and adjustments in the technical process and form independent opinion on workability of plant and machinery and other items.

Basis of valuation

There are several bases for valuation. The familiar methods of valuation in general use are based on either asset values or earnings of the business or a combination of both.

Asset Value

In valuation based on asset value, your experts will assess the open market value of freehold land and building. The market value of the unexpired period of leasehold property will also be assessed. The experts will also assess tangible assets like inventories and machineries and also intangible assets like goodwill. They will then value them as per the existing business practices. The existing practices vary from business to business.

Capitalized Earnings

If you want to base your valuation on earnings, the most popular method to use is the predetermined rate of return you expect in routine course on the investment. This is simple rate of return on the capital you invest to purchase the business.

Market Value

This will be applicable only if you are buying a listed business. Market value is the value quoted for the listed business' shares at the stock exchanges. This value however does not exactly reflect the real worth of the business. It takes into consideration various intangible factors such as management abilities, industry prospects, locational benefits, etc which cannot be measured. If you want to arrive at a fair value using this basis, you must ensure that temporary factors such as volatility or fluctuations are eliminated by averaging quotations over a period of time. You should not consider this basis as a good measure of valuation unless there is a broad market for the business' shares. You can rely on it along with the valuation arrived at on the basis of net assets or earnings.

Investment Value

Investment value signifies the cost incurred to establish a business including the original investment made by the owner plus interest accrued thereon.

Book value

Book value represents the total worth of assets after depreciation but with revaluation. This may present a fair and equitable basis for determining the price you should pay for the business.

Reproduction cost

This method is based on assessing the current cost of duplicating the properties of the business or constructing a similar one. It does not take into account intangible assets. This basis is a good method of valuation for preliminary negotiations.

Besides the above basis, there are other bases also. The three most popular bases globally are asset based valuations, earning based valuation and market price valuation.

Valuation methods for listed and unlisted businesses vary. Shares of listed businesses are quoted at stock exchanges and are available easily. You can buy and sell these shares at the stock exchange. The market price of the shares reflects their value. It is presumed that all relevant information about the business is available to the investors which is reflected in the market price. However you must not completely rely on market price of shares for two main reasons:

1. Correct information about the business may not be available to the investors.
2. Insider trading could cause distortions in the market price.

When it comes to unlisted businesses, business analysis including the shareholding pattern, voting rights, etc along with industry analysis such as the nature of the industry, competition, etc should be considered in valuation.

Valuation based on earnings

Valuation based on earnings is a popular method for valuation. The predetermined rate of return expected by an investor on investment in the business is used to which is equal to the simple rate of return on the capital invested. From the last declared earnings of the business, items such as tax, preferential dividends, etc are deducted and the net earnings are taken for calculation. You should remember that this valuation is based on past performance of the business whereas for fair valuation, reliable forecast of future earnings is necessary.

Earnings analysis

Earnings per share (EPS) is the earning attributable to shareholders which is reflected in the market price of the shares. This (P/E) relationship is known as Price Earning Ratio.

P/E Ratio is calculated by dividing current price of shares (P) by EPS or P/EPS. A higher P/E ratio indicates that the business's earnings in future will grow whereas a low P/E ratio indicates stagnancy in the earnings in future. A reciprocal of this ratio (i.e.EPS/P) depicts yield. Share price (P) can be determined as P = EPS X P / E Ratio

Or P = $\dfrac{\text{EPS}}{\text{Earning yield}}$

While planning for takeover, P/E ratio plays significant role in decision making for the acquirer inter alia, in the following ways:-

(i)   Target Business's P/E ratio is exit ratio and higher the ratio means the acquirer has to pay more. If the exit ratio of target business is less than that of the acquirer then shareholders of both companies benefit. On the other hand, if P/E ratio of target business is higher than acquirer merger will lead to dilution in EPS and adversely affect share price.

(ii)   In share – for share exchange, a business can increase its EPS by acquiring another business with a P/E ratio lower than its own provided that the earnings of the target business are capitalized at a rate above its existing capitalization rate. The above principles are exemplified as under:-

Example A:
    In the following Table 1, the left hand side shows data of companies, A (Acquirer business) and T (Target business) before acquisition. A acquires T at share – for – share exchange. In the right hand side combined earnings of A and T per share after T's acquisition by A are given.
    The share exchange ratio has been calculated as under:-
    T's market capitalization =
    = No. of shares of T x share price of T
    = 5,000 x 15 = $ 75,000
    T's shareholders will receive $ 75,000 worth shares in A at A's current share price of $ 20 per share, i.e. 75,000/20 = 3750 shares.
    Or on T's selling shares at $ 15 to A, the exchange ratio will be 15 + 20 = 0.75 shares of business A's stock for each share of business T's stock. In total 3750 (.75 x 5,000) shares of business A will need to be issued in order to acquire business T. (Total No. of shares in combined business will be 10,000 + 3750 = 13750).

Table 1[2]

	Before Takeover		After Take Over
	Acquirer Business (A)	Target Business (T)	Combined (A+T)
No. of shares	**10,000**	**5000**	**13,750**
Total Earnings	**100,000**	**50,000**	**150,000**
EPS	**10**	**10**	**10.91**
Share Price (MPS)	**20**	**15**	
P/E Ratio (P/EPS)	**2:1**	**1.5:1**	
		(Exit Ratio)	

Now, impact of merger on A's shareholders can be calculated. On the basis of EPS at $10.91 of the combined companies (A + T), the share price of combined undertaking can be calculated by multiplying combined EPS 10.91 by P/E Ratio of A (2:1) i.e. $ 10.91 x 2 = 21.82 which clearly shows a gain of $ 1.82 per share to shareholders in business A, over the earlier pre – merger market price of $20.

The impact of merger on T's shareholders can also be analysed as under:-
= Market Exchange Ratio for T's shareholders = 15 + 20 = 0.75

---

[2] Table obtained from notes prepared by Attorney R.B. Vakil of Mumbai, India. Attorney Vakil is a corporate attorney and a part time professor of law.

= New EPS 0.75 x 10.91 = 8.182.

Shareholders of target business have not gained as EPS has declined by 1.82 per share. A's shareholders have gained in the combined business from the merger because as stated in principle (i) above the exit P/E ratio of the target business is less than that of the acquirer.

Suppose business T demands a price of $ 22 per share instead of $15 per share then $ 22 + 20 or 1.1 share of A for each share of T. In total (1.1 x 5,000) or 5,500 shares would have to be issued and Earning Per Share after merger of the combined business would be $1,50,000 + 15,500 or $ 9.67. This shows dilution in business A's EPS on account of acquisition of T by Re. 0.33 per share. Price earning ratio of A's stock had worked out at 2:1. Share price for combined business comes out to 9.67 x 2 = 19.34 which shows a decline in the share price of the combined business because the PER of target business was more that the acquired business.

Limitation of earning analysis

In the above example, a short – term view of the problem has been taken on the assumption that target business's earnings are capitalized in the market at the higher P/E Ratio. If this assumption is relaxed and weighted average of earnings of companies A and T are taken, then the impact on the shareholders gain or loss could be assessed as under:-

Weighted average of the combined earnings of A and T = (2 x 10,000) + 15,000 + (1.5 x 5,000) + 15,000 = 7/3 + 1/2
$$= 1.8$$

Market value of combined business (A & T) = 10.91 x 1.8 = 19.64

With existing exchange ratio at (15+20) i.e. 0.75, the market value for target business's shareholders would be 0.75 x 19.64 = 14.73 as against $ 15 per share. It means that the shareholders of either business have not gained even with the use of weighted average of capitalization ratio based on earnings.

The results obtained, in short – term, are based on current earnings which are not much reliable. The growth of the business is reflected in future earnings and without taking into consideration the future earnings, valuation is misleading. Therefore, earning forecast for the future is prerequisite for fair valuation. Besides, there are other factors which affect the earning based valuation and deserve financial analysts attention.

Factors affecting p/e ratio

The following factors affect the earnings based valuation.
(1)　Risk – Higher risk results in higher earnings yield and gives a low P/E ratio and vice versa.
(2)　Abnormal growth – Higher abnormal growth gives a low earning yield and higher P/E ratio i. e. it depicts elements of low risk.
(3)　Random fluctuations in earnings affect the P/E ratio i.e. fall in earnings leads to fall in share price causing P/E ratio move up and a rise in earnings causes a rise in share prices and fall in P/E ratio. To avoid the impact of fluctuations maintainable earnings are used in place of current earnings.

Valuation based on assets

Valuation on assets basis of unlisted business is done on different footings as compared to listed businesses. The real value of the assets may or may not be reflected in the market price of the shares. You should apply the following criteria for valuation of unlisted businesses:
1. Fair value
2. Open market value

Fair Value

This criteria may be appropriate when the market value of the business is independent of its profitability. Fair value represents shareholders proportionate ownership of the total value of the entire business.

Open Market Value

This refers to a price of the assets of the business which could be fetched or realized by negotiating the sale provided there is a willing seller, property freely exposed to market, sale could be materialized within reasonable period and throughout this period orders will remain static and without interruptions. The assets of the business which cannot be thus sold is assessed on depreciated or replacement costs. Each asset of the company is normally valued on the basis of liquidation as resale item rather than on a going concern basis. Intangible assets like goodwill will also be assessed as per the normal industry practices.

When you are done with the valuation, you need to make your offer and if your offer is acceptable to the buyer, you will need to get the paperwork done. This is known as closing. Once closing is complete, you will be the proud owner of the business.

Closing

After finding the business, due diligence and valuation comes the closing which completes the deal. The seller knows everything about the business and as such has an extra advantage. Hence it is essential that you find out as much as possible during the due diligence prior to closing. Once you transfer the money, it will be very difficult to rectify even a small mistake. The deal is completed or closed when certain conditions are met within a fixed time. If the conditions are not met within the fixed time, the deal fails.

As a buyer, the closing is the moment most anticipated in the entire process. With closing, the seller legally transfers the ownership of the business to you. From that moment onwards, you are the owner of the business. If things go well, closing will be over within minutes.

The closing is usually done at the office of the buyer's attorney. The documents are signed and the buyer hands over the money to the seller.

Your attorney will play an important role in preparing and reviewing all the documents required at the closing. It is therefore important that you hire an experienced lawyer. The most important amongst all the documents is the Purchase Agreement. This is the document which will transfer the business to you and will provide the terms and conditions of the sale.

Purchase Agreement

Purchase agreement is an agreement executed between you and the seller. It contains the terms and conditions of the sale. This is probably the most important document you will sign concerned with the business. You must ensure that the agreement to the extent possible must be drafted by your attorney. The owners of the business should be made a party to the agreement even if the business that is being purchased is a corporation. Make sure to list all the items being sold in the Exhibit to the Agreement.

If you are assuming any liability or taking over a contractual obligation, make sure that it s listed in agreement separately. Bear in mind that the seller will attempt to list every liability he is aware of, since you won't be bound by any that aren't listed.

While your attorney is drafting the agreement, make sure that there is a holdback provision. This will protect you if you end up having to pay a debt the seller didn't disclose. You will be able to deduct the amount paid from the amount held back at the closing. Generally in the holdback clause, the buyer's attorney is appointed as the escrow agent.

Once you sing the purchase agreement, you are obligated to go through with the deal. After the purchase agreement is signed, if the seller refuses to turn over the business on the date agreed in the agreement, you can sue the seller. The seller can sue you if you fail to make payment of the purchase price as agreed. If the deal does not come through by the agreed date, each party is free to go his separate way.

The most important part of the purchase agreement is the seller's representations and warranties. If the seller fudges on a representation or warranty, it is a breach of contract. If anything said turns out not to be true and ends up lowering the value of the business, you can hold back the part of the money that has not been paid or sue to recover what has been paid.

Lease Assignments

If any of the assets of the business is leased and you are buying those assets as a part of the sale, then you must make sure that the lease is assigned to you. This is because the original lease will be between the seller and the landlord. Lease assignment is a document executed between you, the Seller and the landlord. The Seller will be assigning the lease to you. The landlord will have to consent to the assignment. The document has to be signed by all three parties. The landlord will generally want to meet you before signing this document. The landlord may have a standard form that they use. If they don't, your attorney will prepare one for you. It's a fairly simple document. Make sure you inform the landlord in advance about the closing date. Generally the landlord will not charge you anything to assign the lease except for any out-of-pocket expenses. Sometimes the landlord will not consent to the assignment. Instead they will insist on the signing of a new lease. They may charge a fee to do so.

Landlords need an assurance that the rent will be paid on time. Some landlords may require the Sellers to remain on the lease as a guarantor for the remainder of the term. In such cases you may be required to execute an indemnity in favor of the seller for the guarantee.

Promissory Note

This is the note between you and the lender. The lender may be the seller or another third party. This note is drafted by the lender. This note will be your personal guarantee to repay the debt. If the seller is the lender, while you may be signing personally, you should not pledge any personal assets or security.

You want to have the right, but not the obligation, to pay off the entire amount at any time before the end of the term without penalty. Payments to begin 30–180 days after the closing date and then shall be due each month by the last day of the month.

Reserve the right of "set off" for any liabilities that may arise of which you were not aware at the closing.

Non-Compete Agreement

Non-Compete Agreement is the agreement that will prevent the Seller from becoming a competitor to the business in any manner whatsoever, either as an owner, employee, investor, consultant, etc. This agreement must be drafted by your attorney. This is essential to protect your business from competition. If your seller joins a competitor as an employee or consultant or is connected with the competitor is any manner, it could be detrimental to the business.

Agreement to Co-operate

You will need this agreement to ensure that the Seller agrees to co-operate should anything arise after closing that was overlooked including any unpaid bills, claims, etc. There are many areas in which you will need the seller's assistance even after you become the owner of the business. You may need the seller's assistance in dealing with the existing employees and customers.

Lien Search and Filings

These are the documents that will provide proof that all assets are free and clear as per the agreement. Where necessary, liens will be filed against the assets pledged as security for the loan you have availed from the lender

Before the closing, make sure you know the inventory levels of the business. The seller will not be there to order them for you. Collect everything from the seller.

Upon successful completion of the closing, the business is all yours. Congratulations.

Sick Business

Sometimes you may come across a sick business which is up for sale. Should you just ignore it because it is sick or should you give it a good look? Not all sick businesses are dead businesses. They can be revived by carefully planned actions.

So should you buy a sick business? The answer to this question is another question- Why not?

The business is sick. It can't get any worse. So you will get the business at a rock bottom price. With a well planned corporate turnaround strategy, you can successfully turnaround the sick business, return the business in profit, grow the business and exit from the business if you feel like. However corporate turnaround is not for everyone.

Turnaround

Sometimes the business you takeover or buy may not be in the best of shape. It may be a sick business and its very existence may be threatened. Only timely intervention on your part can save the business. You will have to do all you can and engineer a corporate turnaround of the business.

What is a corporate turnaround? A corporate turnaround is the turnaround in the economic and financial fortunes of a business. Before the turnaround, the business will be in the dumps and its very existence will be under threat. With corporate turnaround, all that will be a thing of the past and the business can look forward to economic and financial recovery. A corporate turnaround does not necessarily mean that the business will achieve tremendous economic and financial success. It could involve mere survival with financial results that are acceptable to the owners of the business.

Preparing to buy a sick business

When you buy a sick business, you must identify appropriate strategies for the survival of the business and plan accordingly. You must embark on a fact finding mission. This is the first step in the corporate turnaround process. Once all the facts are gathered, you must diagnose the scope and severity of the problems of the business.

When you buy or takeover a sick business, it is important for you to consider whether the business justifies its existence. Accept the fact that the business is sick. A sick business, if it has to turnaround needs immediate assistance. The ability to detect and act quickly to solve problems is important for the success of the turnaround.

Make a diagnostic assessment of the situation the business is in. The seriousness of the situation should be utmost on your mind. Try and find out the reasons for the sickness of the business. Assess the strengths and weaknesses of the business.

To turnaround a sick business, firstly your mission must be very clear – to turnaround the business. You should have the intention to turnaround the business. Your objectives should be clearly defined. You should work on achieving those objectives. There may be times when you will have to take some tough decisions which may not be to everyone's liking. You need to be prepared to take those decisions.

The important factors that are necessary for a successful corporate turnaround are:
1. Intention – You should have the intention and willingness
2. Control and flexibility – If you are going about the turnaround all by yourself, you should have absolute control. If you are hiring a professional for the job, make sure you give him enough flexibility.
3. Finance – Finance is very important for turnaround. It is essential that you have the necessary finances and resources for the job.
4. Employees – Employees play an important role in the turnaround process. Without their support turnaround will not be possible. You should motivate them and ensure their support for your turnaround plans.

Finances

Like in any business deals, finance plays an important role in the turnaround process. You should make sure that you have sufficient finances to turnaround the business. If you run out of finances, you may have to abandon your turnaround plans. Look before you leap should be your motto. Take stock of your finances and analyze how long your finances can sustain the business. One of the main reasons for a business becoming sick is the financial drain. You must reduce the financial drain and at the same time look at ways to increase the finances of the business.

Finance is the lifeline of any business. You must as soon as possible establish a positive operating cash flow. You must have cash to implement the turnaround process.

Downsizing

Generally to turnaround, a sick business must scale back and downsize. You should review the products or services of the business that account for majority of the sales and profit. Products and services that do not contribute to the revenue and is a burden on the resources of the business must be discarded.

Although a very sensitive issue, employee lay-off is another unavoidable aspect of turnarounds. It is inevitable that you will have to ask some employees to leave the business. It may not be a pleasant thing but if you want to turn around the business, you will have to do it. You will have to take some tough decisions to make the turnaround work. Lay off employees who contribute less to the overall productivity.

Intellectual Assets

Analysis the entire working of the business and locate in the business few products, profit centers, or business units, which will support a profitable and reorganized business and fits into your overall turnaround plan. These are intellectual assets, not physical assets, and they are the hidden drivers behind most successful modern companies and are usually a combination of skills, process and knowledge. These can become weapons that you can use to win the battle for competitive advantage. It can be used over a long period of time.

Financials and Inventory

Like in any business, you should analyze the financials of the business for the last 5 years. You can start with the profit and loss statement and try to find out the break even point.

Review the overall sales trends and determine the factors that caused the downfall of the business. Locate the products and services that contribute the most revenue and the biggest customers who account for most of the sales.

You must review the balance sheet for the past 5 years to find out the financial strengths and weaknesses. You should assess the value of the assets and check if they have been valued correctly. Check the account receivables and whether they are dependant upon contract completions or continued business operations. The accuracy of the inventory must be verified. You should also verify if they are owned or leased and if they are saleable or obsolete. Liquidity is very important for the successful turnaround of the business. Your goal must be to generate as much liquidity as possible from receivables, inventories, intangibles and fixed assets. While is it important that you go after the receivables, you should also be careful to ensure that you do not impair your relationship with the customers.

Figure out which assets and inventory is unessential and can be sold. Use the balance sheet to figure out:
- Will slow-payment or non-payment of trade obligations affect continued supply?
- How are overdue payables handled?
- What are the past-due tax obligations?
- What tax collections are threatened?
- Are secured debts and leases current or in default?
- Is foreclosure or repossession threatened on any secured or leased equipment?
- What is owed to pension plans?
- How insolvent is the business?
- How illiquid is the business?

Management Changes

However you may want to look at it, the fact is that the management of the business does have a role to play in its downfall. Had they read the signs properly and taken timely action, it is unlikely that the business would be in the state that it is currently in. The management may not accept this but it is very true. You will have to take some tough decisions here. You should replace the management staff especially those who you feel will hinder the turnaround process. It is essential that the management believe in your plans to turnaround the business. The management should consist of qualified and capable persons who will enable successful turnaround of the business.

Survival Plan

When you buy a sick business, the business would have already hit rock bottom and any further decline will effectively end the business. The very survival of the business is threatened. You should take immediate plans to prevent any further decline of the business. You should have a survival plan ready to prevent the business from sinking further and survive the downfall. The plan should include financial, marketing and operations actions to restructure debts, improve working capital, reduce costs, improve budgeting practices, correct pricing, prune product lines and accelerate high potential products. The plan should be able to overcome the threat to the survival of the business.

Dealing with creditors

Creditors are another important aspect of the turnaround process. How you deal with them is very important. Their support is vital for the turnaround. You will need as much co-operation as possible from them. Here honesty is the best policy. Forget phony excuses. Explain clearly that you are experiencing problems and cannot pay at the moment. Inform the creditors of your turnaround plan and ask for their co-operation. Sit down with them and plan with them to pay them off. Never be intimidated by creditors. They cannot do more damage to the business. The credit rating of the business is already down. It is very important that they believe in your turnaround plan and have faith in your abilities. If they fell that you cannot repay them or they have no faith in your plans, they can throw you into bankruptcy. When discussing with the creditors, make sure that you do not reveal who your other creditors or suppliers. A disgruntled creditor may solicit their aid to throw you into bankruptcy.

Cash Outflow

While cash is very important to keep the business from declining further, excess cash flow can be disastrous. You must get a firm grip on cash disbursements and receipts. You must maintain a strict control on the outflow of cash. For this it is essential that you identify all disbursement mechanisms and ensure that no payment occurs without your knowledge and consent. By understanding and controlling the cash outflows you will be able to identify potential areas for cost reductions. You have to get the message across to the staff and employees that it is not business as usual - the old spending patterns and capital projects must be re-evaluated.

It is vital that you gain a quick understanding of the business and its cash flows. You must determine whether the accounting and reporting system produces the necessary data to produce management reports needed to run the business, and if it accurately captures all the transactions entered into by the business and lists all of its assets and liabilities.

Restructuring

Once you have the survival plan in place including the operating cash flow, your immediate priority should be to restructure the business. One of the factors that could have contributed to the decline of the business prior to your buying the business is that the business could have certain unprofitable and resource consuming divisions. Hive off unprofitable and resource consuming divisions of the business and instead focus all resources on the products and services that generate the maximum revenue and make them as efficient as possible.

Another factor that could have contributed to the decline of the business is that the business had a wrong product mix. Your turnaround process could result in the likely change in the product mix of the business. You may also have to reposition the product in the market.

A turnaround process generally involves plans and strategies to be implemented that entail having to do more with less. Therefore you will not only have to bring about changes in the management but you will also have to change processes to increase productivity. Changing policies and procedures is laborious and requires detailed knowledge of products, delivery systems, personnel qualifications and operating assets. Hire professional help if necessary.

Strategic review

Remember there are many issues involved in a corporate turnaround. It is easy to become focused on one issue and forget another. You cannot afford to do that if you want to turnaround the business. You will often face many tactical challenges. You must concurrently address all issues and conduct a strategic review to articulate a new strategy whereby the business will grow revenues and be cash flow positive. Resist all strategies that require significant new inflows of capital. Remember new debt or equity inflows may not be available to a business that is in the midst of a turnaround.

Marketing

It is important that you market the products of your business well for the turnaround. Only if you sell your products and sell well, will you succeed in getting the cash flow necessary for the turnaround. You must precisely define the market for your business and exit all other markets. One of the most common reason for many businesses going downhill us that their marketing plans were based on outdated or conjectural market data. You must carefully gauge the existing demand for the products and services being offered. Assess the size of the market and the market share of the business. Figure out ways to increase the market share of the business. The findings should be used for correct allocation of capital and personnel resources.

The business must show growth in its core products. It will help send out a message to the customers, creditors and investors that the business does indeed have a future.

Communication

The art of communication is very important in a corporate turnaround. You must convince everyone connected with the business the need for urgency and change. Everything depends in how you convey it. You should convey a need for change without sending a doomsday message. You should also convince the staff that restructuring is necessary for successful turnaround of the business. They should have confidence in you.

Communicating with customers and taking steps to retain their business is key for the turnaround's success. No customers – No business.

In the early stages of the turnaround process, the emphasis is on correcting the problems, arresting further downfall and maintaining cash flow. Once that is done, the emphasis shifts to maintaining a strong balance sheet and strategic efforts including initiating new marketing programs, broadening business base, increasing market share, new products, etc. Once you turn around the business, you can run it like any other business and starting making investments to expand the business.

Conclusion

It is by no means an easy task to around a troubled business. You will need some traits that are rare in today's world - skill, foresight, and perseverance. So it is likely that you will hear of more businesses having failed than those having managed a successful turnaround. There is a lot you can learn from the businesses that have successfully turnaround.

All businesses are run by humans. To err is human. Therefore it is but natural that businesses will also err. However businesses must also learn from the mistakes and should be able to turnaround successfully.

Successful turnarounds

Sears, Roebuck and Co.

Sears, Roebuck and Co. better known as Sears is an example of a successful corporate turnaround. The company had once enjoyed the top place in the US retail business where the customer is the king. However neglect of its customers cost the company its profitability. It lost its focus and the company becoming inward-centric, losing touch with its business environment, which had kept changing all along. As a result it lost customers, frittered away market share and risked its very survival. It had flawed diversification strategy and venturing into several unrelated areas. It failed to sense the changing trend in retail, the area where its core competence lay.

It did however turn itself around. Unsurprisingly, it managed to turnaround by refocusing on its customers. It made all its operations geared toward them. Sales people and ambience were made customer-friendly to bring their lost customer base back to the stores.

In an effort to turn around, it stopped its all for all attitude and identified core segments and began focusing on its core segments. It took a good look at its competitors and studied the market trends. To ingrain the service philosophy amongst its employees, it started an exercise whereby every employee's appraisal included a measurement for customer service and compensation depended on the performance on that parameter. The efforts paid off and Sears was able to make a successful turnaround.

Sears was able to turnaround because the management was able to recognize the fact that the man of the family was not longer their main customer, instead it was the woman. Everything about Sears began to reflect this.

Marks and Spencer

Marks and Spencer is a UK based giant also in the retail business. To turnaround its business, Marks and Spencer created a central marketing division whose task was to find out what the customer wanted. The data collected was used to develop the stock based on the requirements of the customer. This also enabled them to reduce the wastage of stock as only those products that were required by the customers were stocked.

In its attempt to turnaround, Marks and Spencer realigned its business structure and organization and split its business into 3 parts - UK retail, overseas retail, and financial services. This was done to enable each to operate more efficiently. This also enabled individual problems to be detected and removed.

Marks and Spencer was able to understand the importance of thinking from the customer's perspective. It also changed the appearance of its stores and even began selling online.

IBM

A business's culture can make a business complacent. This could be a recipe for failure. For such businesses to turnaround, it is important that they change their culture. To bring about a change in culture, sometimes, a change in leadership is necessary. IBM is a typical example of this. Lou Gerstner was able to turnaround IBM. When he took over as the CEO of IBM, there were plenty of middle managers and executives who were shortsighted. The first thing he did was to rebuild the leadership team. He also defined a strategy for IBM and change the culture which was created by the very success of IBM.

Lou Gerstner's earlier stint with American Express really came in handy. At American Express, he had authorized the purchase of IBM products and as such understood the difference a customer perspective can make.

After he took over, IBM demanded its managers to work together to enable IBM to become a customer focused provider of computing service. IBM went to the extent of slashing prices on its core products so as to remain competitive. By bringing about a change in its culture, IBM was able to successfully turnaround against all odd.

Mergers, Acquisitions, Takeovers

Other than directly buying an existing business from the seller, you can also become the owner of an existing business by merging your existing business with another existing business. Sometimes the best way for you to expand or grow your business is not to simply buy another business but through mergers and acquisitions. If you do not have an existing business, you can acquire or take over an existing business and become its owner.

Although used in the same breath, the terms merger and acquisition have slightly different meanings.

Merger

Merger is the combination of two or more businesses into one single business where one business survives and the other looses its existence. The surviving business acquires the assets as well as the liabilities of the merged business. Usually the business which survives is the buyer which retains its identity and the selling business is extinguished. Merger is the fusion of two or more existing businesses. All assets, liabilities, and stock of one business stand transferred to the transferee business in consideration for payment in the cash, shares or both.

Acquisition

Acquisition is general sense is acquiring ownership in the property. In business terms, an acquisition is the purchase by one business of a controlling interest in the share capital of another existing business. An acquisition may be affected by:
1. Any agreement with the persons holding majority interest in the management of the business like members of the board or major shareholders commanding majority of voting power
2. Purchase of shares of the business in the open market
3. Making a take over offer to the general body of shareholder
4. Purchasing new shares by private treaty

A takeover is also acquisition and both terms are used interchangeably. Take over differs from merger in approach to business combinations i.e. the process of take over, transaction involved in the takeover, determination of the share exchange or cash price and the fulfillment of the goals of the combination are all different in takeovers than in mergers. The process of takeover is unilateral and the offeror business decides the maximum price. Time taken in completion of the transaction is less in takeover than in mergers.

Purpose

The business which proposes to acquire another business is known differently in different jurisdictions. The common and familiar ones in most jurisdictions are predator, offeror, raider, etc. The transferee business is called the victim, offeree, target, etc.

The purpose for your business to acquire another business depends on the corporate objectives of your existing business. It has to decide specific objectives to be achieved through the acquisition. Possible purposes for acquisition include:
1. Procurement of supplies
- to safeguard the source of supplies of raw material or intermediary product
- to obtain economics of purchases in the form of discount, savings in transportation costs, overhead costs, etc
- to share the benefits of supplier economics by standardizing the materials

2. Revamping production facilities
- to achieve economics of sale by amalgamating production facilities though more intensive utilization of plant and resources
- to standardize product specifications, improvement of quality of product, expanding market and aiming at consumers satisfaction through strengthening after sales services
- to obtain improved production technology and know-how from the target business to reduce costs, improve quality and produce competitive products to retain and improve market share.

3. Market expansion and strategy
- to eliminate competiton and protect existing market
- to obtain new market outlets in possession of the target business
- to obtain new products for diversification or substitution of existing products and to enhance the product range

- to rationalize distribution, strengthen retail outlets
- to reduce advertising costs and improve public image of the target business

4. Financial Strength
- to improve liquidity and have direct access to cash resources
- to dispose of surplus and outdated assets
- to enhance borrowing capacity
- to avail of tax benefits

5. General Gains
- to improve its own image and attract superior managerial talent
- to offer better customer satisfaction

6. Own developmental plans

Types of mergers

Mergers or acquisition depends upon the purpose the acquiring business wants to achieve.

Horizontal merger

In horizontal merger, your business and the business you want to acquire are in direct competition and share the same product lines and markets.

Vertical merger

In vertical merger, your business and the other business are connected to each other. One of the businesses could be a supplier to the other.

Market-extension merger

In a market extension merger, your business and the other business will be having the same products but in different markets. Through such a merger, you can gain a foothold in the other market.

Product-extension merger

In a product-extension merger, two businesses selling different but related products in the same market merge to form a new entity.

Conglomeration

In conglomeration, your business and the other business will have no common business areas.

Friendly merger

When you merger another business into your business through negotiations and with the consent and willingness of the owners of the other business, then the merger is called a friendly merger.

Hostile takeover

When you do not offer the target business the proposal to acquire it but silently and unilaterally pursue efforts to gain controlling stakes in that business much against the wishes of the owners of that business, it is known as a hostile takeover. It is commonly known as raids or takeover raid in most jurisdictions.

There are two techniques used in a takeover raid. The first one is when you give an impression of your intention which is reflected in your action of acquiring shares of the business to gain control of its affairs. The second one is when you tender an offer directly to the shareholders without the consent of the owners of the business. Usually this offer is made for cash. You can gain control of the business by inducing a large number of shareholders to sell their shares to you at the offered price. The offer should be valid for a limited period within which the shares must be sold to you.

Steps to organizing a takeover bid

Remember that your takeover bid may not succeed. The target business will do everything possible to thwart your bid. You must organize your takeover bid in a systematic manner. The following steps are usually taken while organizing a takeover bid.

Collection of relevant information and its analysis

You should collect all possible relevant information on the target business. Once the information is collected, get the same analyzed by experts such as lawyers, tax consultants and accountants. You should maintain confidentiality of the information and its analysis.

Examine shareholder's profile

You should check the register of shareholders and see the profile of the shareholders. You will be able to analyze which shareholder is likely to accept your offer.

Investigation of government records

You should investigate the government records of the business and find out the encumbrances and charges on the business's assets and the indebtedness, if any of the business.

Articles of Association

Examine the articles of association of the business. This will allow you to ascertain the powers of the management, directors, etc.

Representation on the Board

You should try and ensure that you or your representative is on the board of directors of the business. Try and win over some of the other directors. This way you can go in for a friendly takeover.

Obtain necessary approval

Some jurisdictions require that you get necessary regulatory approval before you make a bid for takeover of a business.

Make announcement

Once you have the regulatory approvals and all the necessary information, you should publicize your offer so that the other shareholders are aware of the offer. You can also improve the conditions of your offer.

Information about acceptance

Your offer will be open only for a limited time within which the shareholders should accept or reject it. You should regularly announce the acceptance of your offer so that other shareholders come to know of the responses in favor of your offer and make their own judgments.

Consideration

You should dispatch the consideration for the shares of the target business to the shareholders who have accepted your offer. You should then take necessary steps to transfer the share in your name.

Your offer documents

When you make an offer to takeover another business, your offer document must contain certain information. This information may vary from jurisdiction to jurisdiction but generally the following information will be contained in your offer documents.

General information

General information about your business, your experience, your intention to continue the other business, your ability to successfully run the business, employment of the existing employees, major changes you plan to introduce after the merger or takeover and justification of your offer.

Financial information

You must disclose your means of financing the takeover.

Terms of offer

You should state that you will be acquiring the shares free of all aliens, charges encumbrances, the total consideration offered for the shares in cash or kind, the mode of payment, the basis for arriving at the consideration, duration of offer, condition attached to the offer, etc

Information on your business

Provide detailed information about your business including financial information, shares, market price, status of your business, etc

Profit forecast and asset valuation

You should provide reasonable projections and support it by future growth plans.

Information of the target business

You should provide the details of existing shareholding in the target business and its management.

Arrangement for acceptance

You should spell out the various arrangements you have made for materializing the acceptance such as underwriting arrangements, appointment of merchant bankers, etc.

Locating the target business

First thing you will need to decide is whether the target business will be in the same business as you are in or in another entirely non-related business.

If the target business is engaged in the same activity as your business, your objective should be growth oriented seeking expansion in production and market segments, utilization of existing capacities and optimum utilization of resources.

If the target business is unrelated to your business, merger or acquisition will promote diversification in the production line and exhibit the risk of mismanaging the operations unless all protective measures are ensured.

Once you establish your goals and targets, the search for a particular type of target business should be undertaken. You can plan the search directly or through the services of middlemen such as business brokers and merchant bankers.

If you want to engage the services of a middleman, you must make detailed enquiry about the middleman with reference to its track record, market reputation, integrity, reliability, management and professional expertise.

Role of Merchant Bankers in Mergers and Acquisitions

Merchant bankers are the middlemen in settling negotiations for merger and takeover between you and the target business. The role of merchant bankers is specific and specialized in handling the merger and takeover assignments. Their assistance is useful to both you and the target business. Being a professional expert, merchant banker is apt to safeguard both your interests. Their role covers the following areas:
1. Observance of professional norms
2. Steps to be taken
3. Selection of the method for takeover or merger
4. Financial analysis

Your role

You should maintain strict secrecy of the deal till final settlements are reduced to writing to avoid intervention of other parties, to avoid disruptive transactions in the stock market, to prevent insider trading and to prevent proxy wars at the shareholder meetings.

You should not bypass any statutes or laws. You should also ensure that the target business also does not violate any statutes or laws.

Sometimes violation of statutes or law on part of the target company may devolve upon you.

You should also make financial arrangements for the deal.

Investigation before merger

It is very important that you or your merchant banker carry out the following analysis of the target business before starting negotiations.

(i)   Industry analysis.

Industry analysis shall include the task of collecting macro information and analyzing it to assess prospects of profitability from acquisition:-

- competition within industry and from other industries.
- competitive strategies within industry and from other industries.
- growth rate in industry with reference to sales, profits:
  - external factors affecting growth rate
  - projection for future.
- mergers / acquisitions already taken place in industry. If so, what results whether good for survival of industry and maintaining growth rate.
- competitors in industry and importance of patents, trade marks, copy rights etc.
- Essential elements of success and barriers to entry.

(ii)   Accounting and financial analysis

Following financial and accounting information must be collected for the target company as well as for the industry to have a comparative view:-

- Financial Ratios – Comparison
- return on assets or on net worth
- gross profit
- profit margin
- fixed charge coverage
- assessment ratio

- net quick ratio
- Debt: Equity ratio
- inflation rate or its impact on operation
- current value
- replacement cost data
- future capital requirement
- balance sheet and profit and loss account for past year
- statement of charges in financial position.
- budget and forecasts for future
- difference in accounting buyers and sellers
- over valuation of assets – inventories
- accounting policies, depreciation policies
- bad debts provisions, contingencies, etc.
- taxes:
  - tax status of target company
  - tax liabilities outstanding
  - reserves for tax payment
  - taxing authorities reports

(ii)   Management analysis investigation

To collect information on aspects covering: Management Organization and industrial relations.
- interview senior officers of target company
- review their business experience
- investigate their background
- union contracts – strike history
  - existing problems
  - labor agreements
- personnel schemes
- saving plans and employees benefit plan
- permanent employees, age, qualifications and experience

(iii)   Marketing analysis

Collection of information should cover the following:-
- about sales: Product and marketing factory
- sales, profit, backlog by product line/monthly sales/government sales/ marketing and sales

organization, sales planning and forecasting – advertising and sales promotion, competitive strategies.
- about product: Major product/new product development/obsolete products. Product life cycle and technology.
- About customer: Customer attitude / customer buying power incentive plan/research
- trends: Company/industry and compares within outside the industry

(iv) Manufacturing and distribution: Engineering analysis

Production facility for each, collect following data
- name / location / owned assets / leased assets / book value / fair market value / capacity / employees / present condition / alternative uses.
- manufacturing process
- supplies of major material
- physical distribution method
- research & development
- reporting control – regulatory reporting requirements.

(vi) Miscellaneous information
- Inventory: Distributions like undervaluation to minimise taxes and concealed earnings, over – valuation of inventory, (obsolescence by technological development, changing technology or new product)
- Litigation – liabilities
- Drawing up of financial statements – unearth the tactics
- deferral R & D expenses and repair and maintenance
  - release of inventory reserves
  - unduly low reserves
  - undisclosed changes in accounting methods
  - low estimates of debt, accounting rate of return etc

- Carrying investigation:
  - Receivables not collectible at recorded amount
  - Doubtful accounts / cash trade discounts not adequately recorded.
  - Unrealizable investments: Non – marketable investments be written down.
  - Personal expenses in private company – reduce net income/misleading information
  - Unrecorded liabilities – vacation pay / sales returns / allowance
  - discount / pension liabilities / claim items from loss contracts / warrants
  - Poor financial control / poor pricing / poor costing
  - Few major customers
  - Foreign operations – overseas units pose difficult situation in accounting
  - Unusual transactions – sale of assets taken to improve the trend.
  - Tax Contingencies

(vii) Economic analysis

Those aspects which are not related to target company's operations should be covered particularly with reference to the following:
- competitive conditions
- business cycles
- public reaction / to takeovers
- Government policies., etc.

(viii) Non balance sheet factors

Those factors which have not been covered under above sub-heads should be considered in the analysis like:
- conditions of securities market
- nature of consideration to be offered i.e. (a) Cash offer or (b) exchange of securities offer.

Check list for completing preliminary investigations

1. Memorandum and articles of associations of the target business.
2. Business formation documents
3. Management documents and agreements
4. Directors/Owners loans to the business
5. Audited accounts for 5 years and current year
6. Cash flow and ratio analysis for 5 years with projections for 5 years
7. Recent valuation report
8. Financial analysis for the last 5 years
9. Budgeted accounts and management accounts for the past 5 years covering the current year
10. Staff analysis for the past 5 years including productivity, salary, etc
11. Production costs for the current year and projections for five years
12. Capital requirements for the next 5 years
13. Financial forecasts for the next 5 years
14. Depreciation policy
15. Production – products, plant location, production Techniques
16. Sales – market share, image of the business

Selection of methods for merger or takeover

Based on the information received about the target business and the resources available with you, you can select any one of the following methods which are in vogue for mergers and takeovers:

a) Acquisition for cash of the shares or assets of the target business

You can takeover the target business for cash consideration either for all or in part of all the issued equity capital through a bid directly from the equity holders or through the stock market. You can also have the new shares in sufficient numbers allotted to you or your representatives to gain control of the target business. Alternatively you can also purchase by way of an agreement for cash, of the assets of the target business. Cash may be in the form of currency notes, loan stock or non-convertible debentures.

In most jurisdiction including the United Kingdom, the rule in vogue is that at least 90% of the shareholders of the target business should accept the bid at the stated prices and within the specified time.

b) Acquisition in exchange of shares or other securities

You can bid for all the issued equity share capital of the target business. In exchange for the shares of the target business, you must provide shares of your business to the shareholders. Like cash offer, this is also conditional in most jurisdictions upon acceptance by shareholders of not less than 90% in vale of the shares. The shareholders of the target business will become the shareholders of your business.

Closing

Your merchant banker will prepare a schedule and checklist of the formalities to be completed to conclude the deal. You must keep in mind the following points at the time of closing:
1. For cash transactions, the format of contents of the certificates or letters to be signed by you and the target business
2. For sale of assets, documents such as bill of sale, agreements, sale deed for transferring immovable like real estate, deed of assignment in case of lease and other similar documents to title should be drafted for finalization.
3. Settlement documents for retrenchment or unemployment compensation
4. Documents for transfer of deposits from the account of the target business to your account
5. Delivery of comfort letter on completion of the transaction which must spell out that all procedures have been adhered to.

Synergy

For any merger or acquisition to be successful, integration and synergy are very important. For every completed merger or acquisition, synergy must be created to reach the intended levels of success. The management/owners of the two businesses should work towards melding their businesses' expertise, resources and products towards a single, seamless operation. To achieve synergy, you will have to effectively integrate the assets, operations and personal of the combined businesses. It will require a great deal of efforts on your part. Never commit the mistake of underestimating the magnitude of problems and issues that can accompany the integration efforts. You must make all plans for the integration before the merger. If you fail to achieve integration of the businesses, it contributes to a lack of acquisition success.

You must properly integrate acquisitions into the businesses current operations if synergy is to be created and increase share holder value and competitiveness. One of the main objectives of the integration process is to uncover potential problems that could prevent the combined business from operating in ways that create competitive advantage and value and to determine actions to take that prevent other integration related difficulties. You can improve the probability of successful integration by acting quickly. If you fail to act quickly enough to integrate the businesses together, you will destroy the value the businesses hoped to create in the first place.

The employees of your business and your target business play an important role in the integration. You must remember the employees of each business have their own set of beliefs and culture and if you are not careful, there could be a clash between the beliefs and culture of your business and your target business. The employees of your target business not only have to abandon their existing beliefs and culture but also have to accept a new one which could result in the feeling of hostility and thereby reduce their commitment and co-operation, both of which are necessary for a successful merger. The hostility could result in an 'us versus them' situation between the employees of your business and your target business which can be detrimental to the merger.

If the compensation in the target business is lesser compared to your business, employee expectations could give rise to a possible hike in compensation which may not be realistic. If the compensation level of employees in the target business is lower, the employees may press to have equal compensation across business.

You must have a clearly defined communication strategy. A clearly defined communication strategy plays an important role in removing the employee fears and kill rumors floating around in the business. You must reach the employees. For your communication strategy to be successful, it is necessary that you involve the senior management of the target business as well as other employees who are trusted by the employees for instance trade union leaders are also helpful.

Operations

You can create synergy by effective matching of organizational capabilities of the two businesses. There are endless ways of doing this. If you combine businesses that are both strong or weak in the same business activity, the chances of creating the synergy that leads to competitive advantages and enhancement of shareholder values is limited. As such your business could end up with the same strengths or weaknesses. You can integrate the functional activities of the newly formed business which can result in operational synergies through economies of scale and/or scope.

Research & Development

You can achieve synergies in R&D and technology. You can link activities associated with R&D processes and the technologies that are often critical to them.

Market

You can successfully create synergy by linking various market related activities including those of brand names, distribution, advertising, etc. You must be sufficiently client focused when attempting this to achieve this type of synergy. Trying to cross sell products to customers should be avoided. You can also merge and share the sales force.

Organization

If the two businesses have similar management process, cultures, systems and structures, you can achieve organizational synergy. For this, you must ensure that the two businesses have a high degree of compatibility. The existence of compatibility can result in the expected results being achieved rather quickly, efficiently and effectively.

Once you achieve synergy, the benefits that you can derive from the synergy must exceed the cost of achieving and exploiting it.

Creating synergy is very important for a merger or acquisition to be successful. Creation of synergy increases the probability that a merger or acquisition will facilitate the development of competitive advantages in the newly formed business as well as the generation of value for the owners and especially for stockholders.

You must remember that events occurring within the industry of the business can influence the process of the merger and also its success. You should evaluate this influence within the context of the businesses' capabilities, core competencies, and opportunities. You should exercise even more caution and complete careful and detailed analyses before selecting target businesses if the entire industry is active in terms of mergers and acquisitions.

You should examine the wealth enhancements opportunities through synergy creation permitted by the merger as compared to other opportunities available to the business. Mergers and acquisitions are another means of competing in a complex global economy. Therefore you should evaluate the opportunity costs associated with a merger and acquisition strategy in comparison to the costs associated with other feasible strategic options.

Talking is very important for synergy creation in a merger. You will need to talk extensively and carefully during the negotiation phase about synergy creation. Before you finalize the merger or acquisitions, it is important that all parties are made aware of the type of synergy that can be created and the actions that will be required for that to happen quickly and effectively.

If you go through the various successful mergers and acquisitions, you will notice that the most successful ones are those in which all the foundations of synergy creation exist.

You should try and avoid hubris when evaluating possible sources of synergy between your business and the target business. Synergy is an elusive outcome. To create synergy, you must actively manage organizational process. You can create synergy only through deliberate commitments and actions. Synergy does not happen by chance.

It is also possible to create synergy sometimes through cutting of jobs. However this is a sensitive issue. You must be prudent and wise when evaluating the possibility of job reductions. If you reduce too many jobs, you could end up with a lack of competitive knowledge that is required for long – term effectiveness and efficiency.

Growth through merger and acquisitions

If you want your business to grow through mergers, you will have to decide on whether you want to be an active acquirer or a casual acquirer.

If you are a casual acquirer, consider only those mergers and acquisitions that represent highly positive opportunities. Refrain from actively pursuing acquisitions. You should focus your attention on other managerial issues such as innovation and internal operations. If you do find a target business that is highly desirable, you must make good use of merger and acquisition experts. This will enable you to limit the number of mistakes you can make in the process and will also ensure a successful merger.

On the other hand if you are an active acquirer, consider acquiring businesses that are strategically similar to those that you have already acquired. You can use all the knowledge and experience gained from earlier mergers and acquisitions. It will be most relevant. In business, industry familiarity facilitates learning.

You should study and learn from the mergers and acquisitions of other businesses especially your competitors. Your personal contacts and the various trade and business magazines can provide you with a wealth of valuable information.

It is important that you provide visible and tangible support of the merger process. You must take deliberate steps to promote the merger. You must document, manage and make available all information about the merger. You should assemble a team of merger and acquisition experts who are involved in all your mergers and acquisitions. This will ensure that all knowledge accumulated will be transferred to future mergers and acquisitions. You should treat the merger and acquisition experts as a valuable organizational resource and you should encourage them to remain with your business.

Always remember that even if you follow all the steps necessary for a successful merger and acquisitions, there is no guarantee that your actions will result in General Electric type acquisitions performance; however, they are a step in the right direction.

Has a sick company been turned around by merger?

The year 2001 was a year of depressed sales and earnings in the information technology industry, with many high-tech companies forced to slash their workforces as demand shrivels. Two computer manufacturing companies – Compaq and HP were facing decreased profits and a slump in demand for their products. The two companies decided to merge and bring about synergy in their operations and products. With the merger, the two companies were able to successfully halt their downward slide and manage their business better. Today the merged entity has displaced Dell as the number one computer company in the United States.

Merger Experiences

General Electric (GE)

Perhaps the best example of a business have grown through mergers is GE Capital Services. GE has managed to successfully achieve integration with all its mergers and this has resulted in a core competence. GE Capital is a financial conglomerate with 27 separate business, more than 50,000 employees worldwide, and businesses that range from private label credit-card services to commercial real – estate financing to railcar and aircraft leasing. It has successfully used it merger and acquisition integration competitive advantage as an important means for its continuing growth. GE's integration process begins even before the merger or acquisition is completed and continues all the way through assimilation.

GE has built a vast portfolio of businesses ranging from financial services to aerospace. GE is perhaps one of the most active acquirers. In fact in one single year they have had up to 47 acquisitions. Among their acquisitions are Marquette Medical Systems and Kemper Reinsurance. Statistically huge conglomerates perform poorly. GE has defied this and has recorded admirable financial success over the years. This is mainly due to the fact that since GE makes so many acquisitions, its executives have become very experienced and have the expertise to do them better.

The former CEO of GE, Jack Welsh said that the thrust of GE was to get into the right businesses, find businesses with growth, get an organization that could respond to change quickly and get as much out of the capital invested as possibly can. [3] GE's purchase and subsequent integration of reinsurance businesses from Europe shows its skill and expertise with acquisitions. GE acquired and added Employers Re to its GE Capital group. Employers Re's transformation into a global player was complete through several European acquisitions such as Frankona and Aachen. GE hired a European as the chairman of Employers Re in order to assimilate the European acquisitions into the parent company. GE also hired another European for integrating the European operations.

---

[3] Fortune, December 1997

GE also realized that the naming of the European companies was very important and named the consolidated European companies as ERC Frankona. ERC signified its global presence and Frankona its European heritage. Although GE hired local managers and allowed them to do all that was required to make the integration a success, it conducted regular reviews.

Zeneca and Astra

Many experts look at the merger of equals between pharmaceutical giants Zeneca of the United Kingdom and Astra, a Swedish firm as an example of a transaction that lacked synergy. It lacked synergy in two key performance areas – research and development and managerial skills. Although the merger resulted in greater scale for the two companies, experts felt that it did not solve problems with both companies' medium term pipeline of products needed to replace big-selling drugs that were set to expire early in the twenty-first century.

Glynwed and Friatec

Glynwed based in the United Kingdom is now the world's leading plastic pipe systems business. It consolidated its market position by acquisition of a German company called Friatec. This particular acquisition happened to be the largest ever acquisition by Glynwed. Experts feel that in one go, Glynwed become the world leader in the industry. Besides giving Glynwed a strong hold in the German market, this acquisition also gave Glynwed entry into Eastern Europe, Brazil, and the United States. It acquisition also allowed Glynwed to explore new businesses such as gas and fresh and wastewater. Glynwed was able to achieve synergy by combining the purchasing functions and integrating some manufacturing operations of the two businesses.

Rohm & Haas and Mortin International

Philadelphia based manufacturer of chemicals, Rohm and Haas has always pursued an acquisition strategy to increase its revenue and improve financial performances. Rohm and Hass manufactures chemicals that are found in products such as paints, shampoos, and semi-conductors. To achieve its objective, it purchased Morton

International Inc at the cost of $ 4.6 billion. The target company, Morton International Inc was known mainly for its salt business. It also produced multiple specialty chemicals, including sodium borohydride, which is a bleaching agent used in the newspaper industry to make news pages whiter. The chemicals manufactured by Morton International Inc are also used to increase the quality and performance of end products. The integration of Morton International Inc's technologies and technological capabilities with those of Rohm and Haas extended Rohm and Haas technology platform beyond its premier position in acrylic chemistry and electronic materials and added significant expertise in urethanes, powder coatings, plastic automotive coatings and inorganic chemistry.

NEBS and McBee

In 1998, New England Business Services Inc (NEBS) acquired McBee Systems Inc and McBee Systems of Canada Inc from ROMO Corp. The main reason for the acquisition was the sale force of the target businesses. Combining the sales force of the target businesses with its existing sales force created synergy by allowing NEBS to establish personal selling relationships with small businesses. NEBS possessed a competitive advantage in terms of direct-mail customer relationship. The synergy between this advantage and the target businesses' personal selling relationships competitive advantage would create significant value.

Selling your business

Selling your business could be the most important financial deal you'll ever make. It could also be emotionally very difficult as you have spent years building your business to what it is today. It is unlikely that you will have any previous experience to draw up on unless you have sold another business previously.

It is very important that you should carefully assess your reasons for doing so before you actually sell your business. You must look at your objectives as the owner of the business and the objectives of the business. It is also likely that there will be others who might be affected by your decision to sell your business. This includes your family members, employee and managers.

There are many ways in which you can sell your business. You can like in most cases sell in a trade sale to another business or find a private equity buyer.

Sale options

When you are selling your business, you have different sale options:

Partial or full sale

You can either sell the entire business or make a partial sale. Sometimes the buyer may want you the seller to retain partial ownership and continue to run the business so that they can get the confidence that the business will do well.

Sale of assets

Another option available to you is to sell assets such as equipment, intellectual property or your customer list rather than the business itself. Sometimes, the buyer may find this more attractive especially those who do not want to take on the liabilities and obligations of your business. In such a sale, you will be left with whatever assets and liabilities are not included in the sale.

Payment

Once the sale is completed, you can either get the payment

1. in full or
2. in installments.

Most buyers prefer installments. It might not be in your interest to accept payment in installments. In case the buyer defaults, there you will be at risk.

How to successfully sell

To sell your business the most important thing is that there has to be a buyer for your business – someone who is willing and ready to pay for it. It is important that you identify strong reasons that can easily be substantiated as to why your business would make a good buy. If you fail to identify the reasons, it is unlikely that you will be successful in finding a buyer for your business.

You must first determine if you business is healthy and financially sound. If not, your buyer might not offer you the price you want and will try to buy the business at a distress price.

You should start planning the sale well in advance so that you have time to groom the business and make it as attractive as possible to potential buyers. It is advisable to get a preliminary valuation before you offer it for sale.

Timing

It is important that you sell your business at the right time. This can have a significant impact on the price you get for your business.

The general state of the economy is a key factor. Also the state of the industry your business is in also plays an important role. Buyers would be more willing to buy your business when their own business is doing well. The interest rates and lending practices of banks are also important. You should aim to sell when profits increasing and look likely to grow further. Tax consequences and any forthcoming changes to tax rules also play a role in determining the right time to sell your business.

Choose advisers to sell your business

Your advisors play an mportant role in the sale of your business and can have a big impact on the success of the sale. Effective sale requires experienced advisors. You will need the services of the following:
Accountants
Lawyers

Accountant will look after the financial aspects and preparation of the accounts while the lawyer will look after the legal issues. You may also need a tax specialist to look after the tax issues and to handle business and personal tax planning. A good team of advisors will manage the entire sale process and you can concentrate on running the business.

Before you hire the advisors, you must examine advisers' skills and expertise carefully. They should be experienced of successfully selling similar businesses and they should be able to provide you with references. Above all it is necessary that you are comfortable dealing with them. Before you hire them, settle the fee aspect with them. No one will want to work for free. Try and negotiate a success fee as part of their payment so that you can pay lower fees if you don't achieve your target price.

You may have your team of advisors ready but the most important person in the entire process of selling your business is the buyer. You need to deal with the buyer carefully and convince him that the price you are expecting for the bus ness is the right price for your business and that your business is the business that he is looking for.

The Buyer

Your ideal buyer should be one who does not compete for your ongoing business, presents the least hassles after the sale and offers you the best price for your business. Since there is a chance that you might have to work for him during the transitional stage after the sale, it is important that you get along with the buyer.

Negotiating with the buyer

Negotiate in secret. Don't let your customers, suppliers, and employees find out a transfer is in the offing.

If you're determined you never want to think about this business again and certainly don't ever want to reenter it, you should try to hold out for an all – cash sale. If you do, you'll undoubtedly have to accept a lower sales price. But even if you sell the business for cash, it doesn't mean you're out for good. Along the line, you may have personally guaranteed some of the business's debts or pledged your personal assets to secure these debts. Even if the buyer agrees to assume these debts, the buyer's assumption doesn't let you off the hook. You should attempt to get the lender's consent to replace your personal guarantee with your buyer's. If the lender refuses (and the lender may well refuse if the buyer's credit is not be as good as yours), you should demand that the loans you've personally guaranteed be paid at closing. You should go so far as to require that checks be issued to the lender at closing, with the lender returning the promissory note to you marked "Paid". Failing to do so could result in an unexpected disaster should the buyer default on the note.

Most of the legalities in the purchase agreement benefit the buyer, not the seller. After all, it's the buyer who wasn't there while the seller was running the business, who needs to be protected. Most of the representations and warranties run in favor of the buyer. But there's one aspect of the deal the seller must structure with great care: the security that stands behind the promissory note. If the note isn't paid, you can sue the buyer. But if the buyer can't pay on the note, winning a judgment against that person probably won't do you any good. If the buyer goes into bankruptcy, you won't even be allowed to sue. The security you receive is your assurance you will be able to get at least something if the note isn't paid. You need to be careful, and very tough, when negotiating the security.

If you sell the stock of the business, make sure that, at the very least, you retain a security interest in the stock you sell. This will prevent your buyer from reselling the business without your permission. If the buyer wants to resell, you should have the right to qualify the buyer's buyer, to assure yourself that any new owner will be able to pay the note. Taking a security interest in the stock means that, although you've sold the stock, you leave the closing table with the stock certificates, not the buyer. The buyer should receive the certificates and full ownership rights to them only after the note has been fully paid. Your attorney should also file a financing statement with the secretary of state or country clerk, which gives notice to any prospective buyer that the stock can't be sold until your note has been paid.

Even though you have a security interest in the stock, preventing resale until you are paid, the buyer still will control the corporation. Let's assume that 100 shares represents 100 percent of all the stock of the corporation, and you take a security interest in those shares, leaving the closing table with them. What prevents the buyer from turning around and issuing 10 million new shares to himself or herself the day after the closing, in which event your 100 shares represent an insignificant fraction of all the outstanding shares? Nothing, unless your attorney writes an anti-dilution provision into the purchase agreement, preventing the buyer from doing so.

Obtaining a security interest in the corporate stock isn't nearly enough. It doesn't prevent the buyer from reselling the business' assets piecemeal or in bulk, reducing the corporation to a shell and rendering the stock worthless. At the very least, you should retain a security interest in the business' assets, recording the financing statement with the secretary of state or country clerk. Your security interest should tie up not only the assets you sell but any replacement assets (after-acquired property) as well. If the buyer sells a machine (only with your consent, since you'll have a security interest in it), you should have a security interest in the replacement machine. Securing all the assets includes a security interest in the business' accounts receivable. If the buyer fails to pay on the note, you should be able to step in and collect these receivables.

Obtaining a security interest in the corporate stock and the business' assets is fairly standard; the buyer should not have a serious objection. What's far more difficult is obtaining a security interest in the buyer's personal assets, principally the buyer's home. Depending on the type of business you're selling, the buyer's personal assets may be your principal or sole security.

Never bring your ego in the sale. All buyers will be looking at the weaknesses in the business. Don't take it personally. They have to do so to protect themselves. If you want the negotiations to begin, you must let go of your personal feelings. The faster you let go of your personal feelings, the sooner the real negotiations can begin and you can get the best deal. The best deal for your business may not necessarily be the best deal for you. Separate the two and you stand a very good chance of success.

Documents

All buyers will be looking towards the future. Use your hindsight and expertise to make the buyer see the rosy future for the business. Your sound financial statements and books go a long way in this. Present your business to other in such a way that they are able to understand that your business is a viable purchase. You should formalize all your business policies and procedures. The earlier you formalize the better it is for you at the time of sale. Any document which has been formalized just prior to the sale could create doubts in the mind of the buyer. Some of the important business documents include:
1. Employee policy manual – holiday policy, sick leave, insurance, over-time, etc
2. Work procedure manual containing detailed step-by-step instructions on how various tasks in the business is performed.
3. Customer Agreements
4. Current bylaws and articles of incorporation filed with the state
5. Minutes for every major decision
6. All tax returns

Ensure that all the documents are current. Any discrepancy could lead to perceptions of integrity problems which could create problems in the sale. Be as forthcoming as possible.

Serious Negotiations

The serious negotiations will start after the buyer has examined your documents. The buyer will do his best to obtain the lowest price. Be prepared for a lot of negotiations and arguments. Do not lose your cool. The buyer may appear to be totally inflexible, unfair, and unrealistic.

You will have to go through several drafts of lengthy contracts and it may appear that the negotiations are endless. You may need to be flexible at times and change your goals based on the circumstances.

As mentioned earlier, do not take anything personally.

Patience

Once you are done with the negotiations, it is not the end of the deal. The buyer will conduct due diligence of your business, the same way you conducted when you brought the business. The period of due diligence may vary from business to business. Only when the buyer is totally satisfied that your business is a good buy for him, will he buy it.

Conclusion

Can the philosophy of this book be successfully implemented by anyone? This question can be asked in another simpler way - Has anyone ever succeeded in buying a sick business, turning it around and then grow the business by a merger?

The answer to this question is Laxmi Mittal.

Laxmi Mittal- who?

Till the mid 1990's Laxmi Mittal was a relatively unknown Indian businessman. Even in India he was not too well known. Mittal's family was in the steel industry. Today Mittal is one of the largest producers of steel in the world. Recently he took over Arcelor, an a Anglo-Dutch steel giant.

How did Laxmi Mittal grow from relatively unknown businessman to being one of the largest steel producers in the world in so few years? Simple. He just went about buying sick steel companies around the world and successfully turned them around. He went about buying large sick steel companies in Europe and other parts of the world. He then brought about the necessary changes in them and turned them around. He was thus able to grow his business and eventually took over Arcelor. Today his business empire spans the entire world and Arcelor Mittal is today the world's largest steel producer. The conclusion one can draw from the Laxmi Mittal's experience is exactly what this book is about. He would buy sick business, turn them around and has now taken over another big business to grow his business manifold.

Laxmi's Mittal used the exact strategy listed in the book. He would buy an existing business, which in many cases was a sick business and would then turn it around. Ultimately he had enough money to take over his rival Arcelor and become the largest steel producer in the world. It just goes to show that if anyone can with the right planning and strategy achieve the same.

Sample Documents

Letter of Intent

Purchaser's Name
Purchaser's Address
Date

Re: Purchase of _____ (Name of
business)

This letter of intent contains my offer to purchase
_____ (Name of business) including all assets,
liabilities, business opportunities and corporate name.

Upon your acceptance, we will use our best efforts to enter into a
binding Purchase Agreement and consummate the sale prior to
_____ (Date of closing), on the following terms:

1.   Purchase   Price. The   total   purchase   price   shall   be
$_____, payable as under:

(Insert method of payment – escrow, number of installments, etc)

2. Contingencies. The consummation of the sale is expressly
contingent upon (i) the completion, to my satisfaction, of my full due
diligence investigation, (ii) the assignment of the present premises
lease, and (iii) the review and approval of respective counsel. The
Purchase Agreement will contain the usual representations and
warranties relative to financial statements, corporate
status, lack of litigation, etc.

3. Due Diligence. Subsequent to your acceptance of this letter, my
team of experts consisting of my attorney, accountant and tax expert
may review the books, business operations, and records of the
business. We may not contact your premises lessor, suppliers,
customers, or employees without your approval, which shall not be
unreasonably withheld. In the event that the sale is not
consummated prior to _____ (date of closing), any
information derived by myself, or any individual acting in my behalf,

relative to the business shal be retained in strictest confidence and shall not be disclosed, nor may such information be used to your detriment by means of competition or otherwise. This agreement shall be binding upon you and enforceable by you, whether or not a Purchase Agreement is entered into.

4.   Nondisclosure. Until the sale is consummated, or until _____ (date of closing), you hereby agree not to divulge to anyone, without any approva , either the fact of this Letter of Intent or the pending of a sale of the business.

Please sign a copy of this letter signifying your acceptance of this letter and return the same to me at my address.
Yours sincerely,

_____

Accepted: _____ (Seller's Signature)

Purchase Agreement

This agreement is made on _____[date], by _____, _____[name] with _____[his or her or its] principal office located in _____[city, state] ("Buyer"), and _____[name] of _____[city, state] ("Seller").

ARTICLE I.

PURCHASE AND SALE

1.01. In consideration of the mutual promises and conditions contained in this agreement, Seller agrees to sell to Buyer, and Buyer agrees to purchase from Seller, on the terms, conditions, warranties and representations set forth in this Agreement:

(a) the business owned by Seller, being conducted under _____name, located at _____[address] ("the Business");

(b) all of the stock in trade, inventory, and merchandise of the Business as described in Exhibit "A" attached to this agreement;

(c) all of the fixtures, equipment, and other tangible assets of the Business as shown on attached Exhibit "B";

(d) any leasehold interest owned by Seller under the lease for the premises where the Business is located; and

(e) all the trade, business name, goodwill, and other tangible or intangible assets of the Business.

ARTICLE II.

AMOUNT OF PURCHASE PRICE

2.01. The total purchase price to be paid by Buyer to Seller for all the properties, assets and rights of the Business described in this Agreement ("Purchase Price") shall be $_____.

2.02. The Purchase Price is allocated as follows:

$_____ Inventory

$_____ Fixtures & Equipment

$_____ Goodwill, Tradename & Other Tangible Assets

$_____ Leasehold Improvements

$_____ Non-competition Provision

Total:$_____.

ARTICLE III.

PAYMENT OF PURCHASE PRICE

3.01. The total Purchase Price shall be paid as follows:

(a) $_____ has already been paid to Seller by Buyer;

(b) the sum of $_____ in cash, banker's check or equivalent, shall be paid when this Agreement is signed;

(c) the balance of the Purchase Price shall be paid by delivery from Buyer to Seller of a promissory note executed in favor of Seller by Buyer in the form attached as Exhibit "C" for $_____ that will bear interest from the date of its execution at _____ percent per year and be payable in monthly installments beginning on or before _____[date] in the monthly amount of $_____ each. This note shall be secured by a Security interest on the assets of the Business.

ARTICLE IV.

CLOSING

4.01. The closing of the sale and purchase of the Business ("the Closing") shall take place at the law firm of _____, located at _____[address], on or before _____[date], or at such other place and date as the parties may agree to in writing.

4.02. At the closing the Seller shall:

(a) deliver clear and marketable title and ownership to Buyer of all assets subject to this Agreement;

(b) execute the Bill of Sale attached as Exhibit "D" to this agreement;

(c) execute any other documents necessary to finalize this Agreement.

4.03. At the Closing the Buyer shall:

(a) pay all remaining moneys owed to Seller; and

(b) execute any other documents necessary to finalize this Agreement.

ARTICLE V.

REPRESENTATIONS, WARRANTIES, COVENANTS AND AGREEMENTS BY SELLER

5.01. Seller agrees and warrants and represents to Buyer that:

(a) the financial records for the Business, previously inspected by Buyer, contain a full and complete record and account of the financial affairs of this Business and truthfully set forth all liabilities, assets and other matters pertaining to the fiscal or financial condition of this Business through the date of inspection and furthermore, that there have been no material changes in the financial condition of this Business since that time except for transactions normal to this Business;

(b) Seller is the lawful owner of this Business and has good right and due authorization to sell it. At the time of signing this Agreement, Seller neither knows nor has reason to know of the existence of any outstanding claim or title, or interest, or lien in, to, or on this Business except as shown on the financial records of this Business inspected by Buyer;

(c) all fixtures and equipment sold pursuant to this Agreement are free and clear of any lien and/or debt unless otherwise set forth in a written statement from Seller to Buyer;

(d) Seller owes no obligations and has contracted no liabilities affecting this Business or which might affect the consummation of the purchase and sale described in this Agreement that are not shown on the financial records inspected by Buyer and that have not been expressly disclosed to Buyer;

(e) there are no taxes due and owing on account of Seller's operation of the Business for unemployment compensation, withholding tax, social security tax, sales tax, personal property tax, franchise tax, income tax, and other taxes of any nature;

(f) any accounts payable due and owing as of the Closing shall remain the responsibility of Seller and shall be paid promptly as they become due and payable;

(g) no litigation, actions or proceedings, legal, equitable, administrative, through arbitration or otherwise, including but not limited to lawsuits, claims or disputes with employees, customers and vendors, etc., are pending or threatened that might affect this Business, the assets being purchased, or the consummation of the purchase and sale described in this Agreement;

(h) Seller agrees to indemnify and hold Buyer harmless from any and all claims, causes of actions, damages, or debts, including legal fees, resulting from any actions, occurrences or events occurring prior to the Closing;

(i) all mechanical equipment sold pursuant to this Agreement is in good working condition; and

(j) Seller shall provide to Buyer _____ weeks of full-time training in the operations of the Business.

ARTICLE VI.

REPRESENTATIONS, WARRANTIES AND AGREEMENTS BY BUYER

6.01. Buyer agrees and warrants and represents to Seller that Buyer will duly notify all authorities, suppliers, creditors, and/or other entities that Buyer is to be responsible for all liabilities associated with the operation of the Business, including without limitation withholding taxes, social security taxes, unemployment contributions, salaries, and purchases incurred after the Closing, and Buyer specifically agrees to assume such liabilities as of the Closing.

ARTICLE VII.

COMPLIANCE WITH BULK SALES LAW

7.01. At the Closing, Seller will deliver to Buyer a sworn list of all existing creditors of the Business.

7.02. By reason of this list Seller and Buyer agree that notice to creditors under the Bulk Sales law of _____[state] will not be required and need not be given except in respect to any creditors named on this list.

7.03. Any such debt, unless otherwise provided for in this Agreement, is to be paid solely by Seller, and Seller does indemnify and hold Buyer harmless from any and all loss, expense, damage or liability, including counsel fees, that Buyer may incur or become subject to by reason of noncompliance with the Bulk Sales law.

ARTICLE VIII.

TRADE NAME, TELEPHONE NUMBER AND POST OFFICE BOX

8.01. Seller assigns to Buyer the exclusive right to use the trade or business name and Seller agrees not to use, or authorize others to use, this name or a similar name in the State of _____.

8.02. Seller agrees to allow Buyer to assume the Business telephone number, current advertising arrangements, including "Yellow Pages Advertising," and the Post Office Box, if any, currently used by the Business for a mailing address.

ARTICLE IX.

DELIVERY OF BOOKS AND RECORDS

9.01. All books, records, files, documents and papers, including customer lists and all records of the accounts of customers used in the operation of or relating to the Business shall be transferred and delivered to Buyer at the Closing.

9.02. All of these books, records, files, documents and papers shall be available to Seller at any reasonable time for any proper purpose, and Seller has the right to freely examine and to copy all such materials prior to clos ng.

ARTICLE X.

NONASSUMPTION OF LIABILITIES

10.01. Unless otherwise expressly provided for in this agreement, the liabilities and obligations incurred by Seller prior to the Closing are not assumed by Buyer but continue as liabilities and obligations of Seller and shall be solely paic by Seller.

10.02. In the event Buyer is required to pay after the Closing any valid lien, debt, or expense incurred by Seller prior to the Closing Date, Buyer shall have the right to offset any such lien, debt, or expense actually paid by Buyer, which is the valid and legal obligation of the Seller, against any payment owed to Seller by Buyer.

ARTICLE XI.

INDEMNIFICATION OF SELLER

11.01. Buyer will indemnify ard hold Seller and the property of Seller free and harmless from any and all claims, losses, damages, injuries and liabilities arising from or in connection with the operation of the Business after the Closing.

ARTICLE XII.

DEFAULT

12.01. After execution of this Agreement by the parties, default shall consist in the failure of either party to perform its respective obligations and duties and/or a breach of a warranty or covenant in this agreement.

12.02. In the event of default of either party, Seller or Buyer shall have the right to sue for specific performance and/or sue for damages in addition to any other relief provided in this Agreement or attached Exhibits. In a suit for default, reasonable attorney fees shall be recoverable by the prevailing party.

ARTICLE XIII.

COSTS AND EXPENSES

13.01. All costs and expenses incurred in finalizing the purchase and sale described in this Agreement in the manner prescribed by this Agreement shall be paid by Buyer and Seller in the following manner:

(a) Buyer and Seller agree to jointly retain an attorney to prepare the Closing documents and be equally responsible for the attorney fees and expenses incurred in preparation of these documents. This sum shall be due and payable at Closing. Should either party retain an additional attorney to review the documents necessary for the transfer of the Business, the attorney fees so incurred shall be the responsibility of the party retaining the attorney.

(b) Any other Closing costs and expenses shall be paid at the Closing by the parties, Buyer and Seller, in equal proportions.

ARTICLE XIV.

RESTRICTIVE COVENANTS

14.01. The Seller expressly agrees that for a period of _____ years following the execution of this Agreement, _____[he or she] will not, directly or indirectly, as an employee, agent, proprietor, partner, stockholder, officer, director, or otherwise, render any services to, or on _____[his or her] own behalf engage in or own a part or all of any business which is the same as, similar to, or competitive with the Business, which is being sold to Buyer, anywhere within a _____-mile radius from the current location of the Business that is being sold without the prior written consent of the Buyer.

14.02. The Seller shall not for a period of _____ years immediately following the execution of this Agreement, regardless of any reasons or cause, either directly or indirectly:

(a) make known to any person, firm or corporation the names and addresses of any of the customers of the Seller or Buyer or any other information pertaining to them; or

(b) call on, solicit, or take away, or attempt to call on, solicit, or take away any of the customers of the Seller on whom the Seller called or with whom _____[he or she] became acquainted during ownership of this Business either for Seller or for any other person, firm or corporation.

14.03. Should Seller violate any paragraph of this Article, any remaining amounts now due, or which shall become due, from Buyer to Seller shall be considered paid in full.

ARTICLE XV.

GENERAL AND ADMINISTRATIVE PROVISIONS

15.01. Parties Bound

This Agreement shall be binding upon and inure to the benefit of the Parties to this Agreement and their respective heirs, executors, administrators, legal representatives, successors and assigns.

15.02. Assignment

The Seller shall have no right to transfer or assign _____[his or her] interest in this Agreement without the prior written consent of the Buyer.

15.03. Corporate Authority

If any party to this Agreement is a legal entity (partnership, corporation and/or trust), such party represents to the other that this Agreement, the transaction contemplated in this Agreement, and the execution and delivery hereof, have been duly authorized by all necessary partnership, corporate or trust proceedings and actions, including without limitation the action on the part of the directors, if the party is a corporation. Certified copies of such corporate or other resolutions authorizing this transaction shall upon request be delivered at the Closing.

15.04. Use of Pronouns

The use of the neuter singular pronoun to refer to the Parties described in this Agreement shall be deemed a proper reference even though the Parties may be an individual, a partnership, a corporation, or group of two or more individuals, partnerships or corporations. The necessary grammatical changes required to make the provisions of this Agreement apply in the plural sense where there is more then one party to this Agreement, and to either corporations, partnerships or individuals, males or females, shall in all instances be assumed as though in each case fully expressed.

15.05. Applicable Law

This Agreement shall be subject to and governed by the laws of the State of _____. Any and all obligations or payments are due and payable in _____[city], _____[county], _____[state].

15.06. Severability

If any provision of this Agreement should, for any reason, be held to be in violation of any applicable law, and so much of this Agreement be held unenforceable, then the invalidity of such a specific provision in this Agreement shall not be held to invalidate any other provisions in this Agreement, which other provisions shall remain in full force and effect unless removal of the invalid provisions destroys the legitimate purposes of this Agreement, in which event this Agreement shall be canceled.

15.07. Entire Agreement

This Agreement represents the entire understanding of the Parties hereto. There are no oral agreements, understandings, or representations made by any party to this Agreement that are outside of this Agreement and are not expressly stated in it.

15.08. Notices

All notices or other communications required or permitted to be given pursuant to this Agreement shall be in writing and shall be considered as properly given if mailed from within the United States by first class mail, postage prepaid, and addressed as follows:

to Seller: _____

to Buyer: _____

A party may change the address for notice by giving of such change to the other party in writing.

SIGNED, ACCEPTED, AND AGREED TO on _____[date] by the undersigned parties, who acknowledge that they have read and understand this Agreement and the Attachments and Schedules to it and they execute this legal document voluntarily and of their own free will.

Respectfully submitted,

SELLER: _____

BY: _____

BUYER: _____

BY: _____

Exhibit A

Stock in trade, inventory, and merchandise

Exhibit B

Fixtures, equipment, and other tangible assets of the Business

Exhibit C

Promissory Note

Exhibit D

Bill of Sale

Bill of sale of business

For good and sufficient consideration, receipt of which is hereby acknowledged, the undersigned _____ (Name of Seller) hereby sells, transfers and conveys to _____(Name of Buyer):

1. All and singular, the assets, goods and chattels, property and effects, listed in Schedule A annexed hereto, which is incorporated herein and made a part hereof; and

2. The whole of the good will of the _____ (Name of Business) formerly operated by the undersigned which is the subject of this sale.

The undersigned warrants that said assets, goods and chattels are free and clear of all encumbrances, that the undersigned has full right and title to sell the same, and that the undersigned will warrant and defend the same against the claims and demands of all persons.

The undersigned hereby warrants and covenants that the undersigned shall not within _____ years of the date of this instrument engage in the business of _____ within _____.

Date: _____

Seller: _____

Witness: _____

Promissory Note

Date: _____

Borrower: _____ (Insert name of Buyer)

Borrower's Address: _____ (Insert Buyer's Address)

Payee: _____ (Insert name of Seller)

Place of Payment: _____

Principal Amount: _____

Term: _____ (Insert the number of months)

Monthly payment: _____ (insert the amount of each installment)

INTEREST RATE

Annual interest rate on matured, unpaid amounts shall be _____ % subject to the maximum amount permitted by the Laws of _____.

PAYMENT TERMS

This Note is due and payable as follows, to-wit: _____ (_____) [insert number of payments] equal monthly payments of $_____ principal [insert monthly payment amount]. The first such payment due and payable on the 1st day of _____ , 20_____, and a like installment shall be due and payable on the same day of each succeeding month thereafter until the total principal of $_____ principal [insert total principal amount] is paid in full. If each payment is not paid on time, the remaining balance will be subject to interest of _____ % subject to the maximum amount of interest permitted by the Laws of _____

BORROWER'S PRE-PAYMENT RIGHT.

Borrower reserves the right to prepay this Note in whole or in part, prior to maturity, without penalty.

PLACE FOR PAYMENT

Borrower promises to pay to the order of Payee at the place for payment and according to the terms for payment the principal amount plus interest at the rates stated above. All unpaid amounts shall be due by the final scheduled payment date.

DEFAULT AND ACCELERATION CLAUSE.

If Borrower defaults in the payment of this Note or in the performance of any obligation, and the default continues after Payee gives Borrower notice of the default and the time within which it must be cured, as may be required by law or written agreement, then Payee may declare the unpaid principal balance and earned interest on this Note immediately due. Borrower and each surety, endorser, and guarantor waive all demands for payment, presentation for payment, notices of intentions to accelerate maturity, notices of acceleration of maturity, protests, and notices of protest, to the extent permitted by law.

INTEREST ON PAST DUE INSTALLMENTS AND CHARGES.

All past due installments of principal and/or interest and/or all other past-due incurred charges shall bear interest after maturity @ _____% subject to the maximum amount of interest permitted by the Laws of _____ until paid. Failure by Borrower to remit any payment by the 15th day following the date that such payment is due entitles the Payee hereof to declare the entire principal and accrued interest immediately due and payable. Payee's forbearance in enforcing a right or remedy as set forth herein shall not be deemed a waiver of said right or remedy for a subsequent cause, breach or default of the Borrower's obligations herein.

INTEREST.

Interest on this debt evidenced by this Note shall not exceed the maximum amount of non-usurious interest that may be contracted for, taken, reserved, charged, or received under law; any interest in excess of the maximum shall be credited on the principal of the debt or, if that has been paid, refunded. On any acceleration or required or permitted prepayment, any such excess shall be canceled automatically as of the acceleration or prepayment or, if already paid, credited on the principal of the debt or, if the principal of the debt has been paid, refunded. This provision overrides other provisions in this instrument (and any other instruments) concerning this debt.

FORM OF PAYMENT

Any check, draft, Money Order, or other instrument given in payment of all or any portion hereof may be accepted by the holder and handled in collection in the customary manner, but the same shall not constitute payment hereunder or diminish any rights of the holder hereof except to the extent that actual cash proceeds of such instruments are unconditionally received by the payee and applied to this indebtedness in the manner elsewhere herein provided.

ATTORNEY'S FEES

If this Note is given to an attorney for collection or enforcement, or if suit is brought for collection or enforcement, or if it is collected or enforced through probate, bankruptcy, or other judicial proceeding, then Borrower shall pay Payee all costs of collection and enforcement, including reasonable attorney's fees and court costs in addition to other amounts due.

SEVERABILITY

If any provision of this Note or the application thereof shall, for any reason and to any extent, be invalid or unenforceable, neither the remainder of this Note nor the application of the provision to other persons, entities or circumstances shall be affected thereby, but instead shall be enforced to the maximum extent permitted by law.

BINDING EFFECT

The covenants, obligations and conditions herein contained shall be binding on and inure to the benefit of the heirs, legal representatives, and assigns of the parties hereto.

HEADINGS

The headings used herein are for convenience of reference only and they are not intended to have any effect whatsoever in determining the rights or obligations under this Note.

CONSTRUCTION

The pronouns used herein shall include, where appropriate, either gender or both, singular and plural.

GOVERNING LAW

This Note shall be governed, construed and interpreted by, through and under the Laws of _____.

Borrower is responsible for all obligations represented by this Note.

Executed on this _____ day of _____, 20_____.

Borrower: _____

Non-Compete Agreement

For good consideration received, _____
(Insert name of Seller), the undersigned hereby agrees not to directly or indirectly compete with the business of _____
(Insert name of business) and its successors and assigns for a period of _____ years from date of this Agreement.

The term "not compete" as used herein shall mean that the undersigned shall not own, manage, operate, consult or be employed in a business substantially similar to, or competitive with, the present business of _____ (Insert name of business) or such other business activity in which _____ (Insert name of business) may substantially engage during the term of employment.

The undersigned acknowledges that the Buyer or _____ (insert name of business) shall or may in reliance of this agreement provide the undersigned access to trade secrets, customers and other confidential data and good will. Undersigned agrees to retain said information as confidential and not to use said information on his or her own behalf or disclose same to any third party.

This agreement shall be binding upon and inure to the benefit of the parties, their successors, assigns, and personal representatives.

Signed   this   _____   day   of   _____   20____.

Seller: _____

Agreement to Co-operate

This Agreement to Co-operate is made and entered into on _____ (Insert date) by _____, (hereinafter referred to as "Seller") AND _____ (hereinafter referred to as "Buyer").

WHERES

Seller owned and operated a business under the name and style of _____ (Insert name of business)

Buyer has purchased the said business from Seller and paid the consideration

IN CONSIDERATION OF the mutual promises and covenants hereinafter contained and other good and valuable consideration, the receipt of which is hereby acknowledged, the parties hereto agree as follows:

Seller agrees to provide assistance to the Buyer to transfer management and operation of the said business during normal business hours at the location of the business for a period of _____ days following the closing, all without additional consideration payable by Buyer to Seller.

Each of the parties agrees to take whatever actions as may be necessary to carry out the terms of this Agreement following the closing.

IN WITNESS WHEREOF, the parties have caused this Agreement to be executed by their duly authorized representatives as of the day and year first above written

Seller: _____
Buyer: _____

References

A Casebook on Corporate Renewal by Harlan D. Platt and Marjorie B. Platt

A Not-So-Tender Offer: An Insider's Look at Mergers and Their Consequences by Isadore Barmash

Anatomy of a Merger: Strategies and Techniques for Negotiating Corporate Acquisitions by James C. Freund

Better Business Bureau Guide to Wise Buying by Council of Better Business Bureau

Business Valuation Body of Knowledge Workbook by Shannon P. Pratt

Business Valuations: Advanced Topics by Larry J. Kasper

Buying a Business: A Step-By-Step for the First-Time Buyer (The Crisp Small Business & Entrepreneurship) by Ronald J. McGregor and Kay Kepler

Buying a Business: For Very Little Cash by Joseph R. Mancuso

Business Buying Basics: Your Step-By-Step Guide for Safely Buying a Business by Martin H. Bloom

Business Planning for Mergers and Acquisitions (Carolina Adademic Press Law Casebook Series) by Samuel C., Jr Thompson

Buying and Selling Business Opportunities: A Sale Transaction Handbook by Wilfred Tetreault

Corporate Turnaround: A Practical Guide to Business Survival by Pedro Nueno

Corporate Turnaround: How Managers Turn Losers into Winners by Donald B. Bibeault

Creating Value from Mergers and Acquisitions: The Challenges by Sudi Sudarsanam

Discounted Cash Flow: A Theory of the Valuation of Firms (The Wiley Finance Series) by Lutz Kruschwitz and Andreas Loeffler

Due Diligence by Grant Sutherland

Due Diligence for Global Deal Making ; The Definitive Guide to Cross-border Mergers and Acquisitions, Joint Ventures, Financings, and Strategic Alliances by Arthur H. Rosenbloom

Due Diligence, Disclosures and Warranties in the Corporate Acquisitions Practice (International Bar Association Series) by David Baker

Due Diligence: Definitive Steps to Successful Business Combinations by Denzil Rankine, Mark Bomer, and Graham Stedman

Due Diligence by Christopher Carosa and Patrick C. Burke

Due Diligence Handbook by William M. Crilly

Due Diligence Checklists by Curtis Sahakian

Due diligence in securities transactions (Securities law series) by Robert J Haft

Due diligence: Learn how to avoid pitfalls and deal breakers by Joe H Hicks

Due Diligence: The Critical Stage in Mergers and Acquisitions by Peter Howson

Financial Due Diligence: A Guide to Ensuring Successful Acquisitions (Financial Times Management Briefings) by Stephen Bourne

Financial Statement Analysis and Business Valuation for the Practical Lawyer, Second Edition by Robert Dickie

Financial Accounting: A Valuation Emphasis by John S. Hughes, Frances L. Ayres, and Robert E. Hoskin

Guide to Business Valuation by Les Livingstone Ph.D. CPA

How To Buy a Business by Richard A. Joseph, Anna M. Nekoranec, and Carl H. Steffens

How to Buy or Sell a Small Business Including Buying a Franchise by Verne A. Bunn and C. R. Stigelman

How to Value, Buy, or Sell a Financial Advisory Practice: A Manual on Mergers, Acquisitions, and Transition Planning by Mark C. Tibergien and Owen Dahl

International Business Acquisitions:Major Legal Issues and Due Diligence (World Law Group Series) by Michael Whalley

Insiders Guide to the Merger and Acquisitions Business by George R. Horning

Innovative Corporate Turnarounds by Pradip N Khandwalla

Inside the Minds: Mercers & Acquisitions Best Practices: Leading M&A Lawyers on the Due Diligence Process, Structuring the Deal, and Negotiating Purchase Prices (Inside the Minds) by Aspatore Books Staff

Introduction to Business Analysis and Valuation by Krishna Palepu, Victor Bernard, and Paul Healy

Managing the Merger: Making It Work by Philip H. Mirvis and Mitchell Lee Marks

Making Mergers Work: The Strategic Importance of People by Perrin, Foster & Crosby, Inc. Towers and Jeffrey A. Schmidt

Making Mergers Work: a Guide To Managing Mergers and Acquisitions by Price Pritchett

Managing a corporate turnaround: Role of management consultancy services in the revival of small scale enterprises by M. S Chhikara

Mergers & Acquisitions by J. Fred Weston, Samuel C. Weaver, and Samuel Weaver

Mergers & Acquisitions: Managing the Transaction by Joseph C. Krallinger

Mergers, Aquisitions and Takeovers by H.R. Machiraju

Mergers, Acquisitions, and Other Restructuring Activities (Academic Press Advanced Finance Series) by Donald DePamphilis

Mergers and Acquisitions: Creating Integrative Knowledge (Strategic Management Society Book Series) by Amy Pablo, Mansour Javidan, and Strategic Management Society Staff

Mergers and acquisitions: planning and action: A research study and report prepared for the Financial Executives Research Foundation, by Inc Arthur D. Little

Mergers & acquisitions in the 90s: A step-by-step guide (Corporate law and practice course handbook series)

Mergers and Acquisitions Deal-Makers: Building a Winning Team by Michael E. S. Frankel

Opening investment doors with due diligence.(Brief Article): An article from: San Diego Business Journal by Russell K. Smith (Digital - Jul 30, 2005)

Principles of Corporate Renewal, Second Edition by Harlan D. Platt

Principles of Private Firm Valuation (Wiley Finance) by Stanley J. Feldman

Streetwise Business Valuation: Proven Methods to Easily Determine the True Value of Your Business (Adams Streetwise Series) by Heather Smith Linton

Successful Mergers, Acquisitions and Strategic Alliances: How to Bridge Corporate Cultures by Irene Rodgers, Charles Gancel, Marc Raynauld, and Marc Raynaud

Step-By-Step Business Analysis and Valuation: Using Financial Statements to Value Any Business by Krishna G. Palepu, Victor L. Bernard, and Paul M. Healy

Taking Charge: Management Guide to Troubled Companies and Turnarounds by John O. Whitney

The Art of the Turnaround: How to Rescue Your Troubled Business from Creditors, Predators, and Competitors by Matthew L. Shuchman and Jerry S. White

The Business Of Acquisitions And Mergers by G. Scott Hutchinson

The Business Valuation Book by Scott Gabehart and Richard Brinkley

The Complete Guide to Mergers and Acquisitions: Process Tools to Support M&A Integration at Every Level (Jossey-Bass Business & Management Series) by Timothy J. Galpin and Mark Herndon

The Management of Corporate Business Units: Portfolio Strategies for Turbulent Times by Louis E.V. Nevaer and Steven A. Deck

The Mergers and Acquisitions Handbook by Milton L. Rock, Robert H. Rock, and
Martin Sikora

The Morning After: Making Corporate Mergers Work After the Deal is Sealed by Stephen J. Wall, Shannon Rye Wall, and Sharon Rye Wall

The Role of Mergers in the Growth of Large Firms by J. Fred Weston

The Small Business Valuation Book (Adams Expert Advice for Small Business) by Lawrence W. Tuler

The Upstart Guide to Buying, Valuing, and Selling Your Business by Scott Gabehart

Theory of Valuation by John Dewey

Valuation: Measuring and Managing the Value of Companies, Fourth Edition by McKinsey & Company Inc., Tim Koller, Marc Goedhart, and David Wessels

Valuation Methods and Shareholder Value Creation by Pablo Fernandez

Winning at Mergers and Acquisitions: The Guide to Market Focused Planning and Integration by Clemente and Greenspan

www.ingramcontent.com/pod-product-compliance
Lightning Source LLC
Chambersburg PA
CBHW071448200326
41519CB00019B/5657